The Impact of Enter␣␣␣␣␣␣␣␣␣␣␣␣␣␣␣␣␣ ␣
Employment

Terry Van Allen

The Impact of Enterprise Zones on Employment

Terry Van Allen

Austin & Winfield
San Francisco - London
1995

DEDICATION

I dedicate this work to Jack F. Kemp, who inspired my study of Enterprise Zones through his inspiring books, articles, speeches, and United States legislative and executive branches leadership.

AUTHOR'S NOTE

Due to the delays in publishing my manuscript, I wish to describe two major and more recent events in the public policy of Enterprise Zones (EZs) at the federal level. The first is that the Clinton Administration has now designated sites in accord with the earlier 1993 Empowerment Zones legislation. In fact, additional appropriated but unspent grant funds by the U.S. Housing and Urban Development were redirected and added to the original Empowerment Zones program. The federal Urban Empowerment Zones are in Atlanta, Baltimore, Chicago, Detroit, New York, and Philadelphia-Camden. The federal Urban Supplemental Zones are in Los Angeles and Cleveland. The federal Rural Empowerment Zones are in regions of Kentucky, Mississippi, and Texas. The Urban Enhanced Enterprise Communities are in Boston, Houston, Kansas City (Kansas-Missouri), and Oakland. The Urban and Rural Enterprise Communities were designated across the nation, but have no economic incentives. This brings me to the important point that I do describe in this book--how the current Empowerment Zones legislation lacks major incentives for job creation (as it is more of a welfare program than an economic development program), and how there is a great need for additional economic incentives, as concluded from the evidence of my two research studies.

The second major event is that new legislation has been introduced and co-sponsored by Senator Spencer Abraham (R.-Michigan) and Senator Joseph Lieberman (D.-Connecticut), and it puts substance into the current program. The bill (S1252) is entitled the "Enhanced Enterprise Zones Act," and *primarily targets small start-up businesses in raising capital and maintaining cash flow*, as capital is essential to success. Briefly, the bill's seven significant EZ incentives are: (1) a capital gains tax rate of zero on the sale of business stock, property, or partnership interest; (2) an income tax deduction on purchasing business stock; (3) a doubling of the expensing income credit for purchases of plant and equipment; (4) an income tax credit on the cost of construction, renovation, and expansion; (5) regulatory modifications or waivers for businesses; (6) financial incentives for residents in the homeownership of public housing; and (7) financial incentives for residents to provide for public and private school choice. A companion bill is forthcoming in the House. The likelihood of passing a significant EZ bill has greatly increased by the results of the 1994 congressional election. As a final point, my research studies in this book strongly support the framework of this revolutionary bill.

TABLE OF CONTENTS

LIST OF TABLES

LIST OF FIGURES

ACKNOWLEDGEMENTS

I would like to express my gratitude to Dr. Daniel O'Toole (Department of Public Administration and Policy) of Portland State University for reading and editing a draft of this work. I also extend my sincere appreciation to Dr. James Strathman (Department of Urban Studies) and Dr. Thomas Tuchscherer (Department of Economics) of Portland State University, and to Mr. Thomas Aston (Economist, Portland Office) of the U.S. Department of Housing and Urban Development for their support and comments.

My sincere gratitude is extended to Mr. Jonathan Fields of The Oregon Health Sciences University for his support and expertise in statistical analysis. Grateful acknowledgement is extended to Michael Savage and Jack Underhill of the U.S. Department of Housing and Urban Development in Washington, D.C. for the use of their national data base. My thanks also go to the many scholars (as named in Chapter I) throughout the country who gave me advice and encouragement in completing these studies.

Lastly, I express deep gratitude to my wife, Denise, who gave me tremendous moral support in completing these studies, while I worked in a very demanding administrative, policy-making, and academic career.

PREFACE

INTRODUCTION

The objectives of the two empirical studies in this book are to investigate the impact of Enterprise Zones (EZs) on the employment of zone residents. Thus, this book is divided into two parts. Part One includes a national study of 14 states and 60 zones. However, the first two chapters provide the historical, practical, and theoretical building blocks for both parts and studies. Part Two is a single case study of Portland, Oregon.

The author's investigations constitute the "first" national study to evaluate the employment impact on zone residents (Part One), and the "first" single case study on the employment impact on zone residents in Portland, Oregon (Part Two). The single case study serves as both a distinct and comparative study to the results of the national study. The single case study is based on data collected at the end of year 1993, while the national study is based on data collected in 1989. The specific employment data on Portland is mandated by the State of Oregon to be derived and reported each year. This data is comprised of new jobs created and zone residents hired, as well as the sizes and investment dollars of the participating businesses. Whereas, the national data was provided through a U.S. Department of Housing and Urban Development (HUD) survey, and is comprised of unemployment rates, designation dates, and other demographics.

The relative strength, validity, and reliability of these two studies is discussed in the appropriate chapters. The national study utilizes sophisticated analytical techniques on general unemployment rates, while the single case study provides basic information on specific employment numbers. The author has some recommendations on improving the methodology of the national data collection by HUD, while he highly recommends mandating and expanding upon the precise data collection of the single case study on Portland to all EZ programs.

Part One is comprised of Chapters I through VI. Chapter I gives a historical and up-to-date background of EZs, which describes the important evolutionary and revolutionary aspects of EZs. Chapter II gives the economic principles of EZs, and discusses the criticisms and the scholarship associated with EZs. Chapter III presents the hypotheses and the research design of the national study. Chapter IV reviews and discusses the data frequencies of the national study. Chapter V reveals the results of testing the hypotheses, and discusses the employment impacts and variables of EZs. There are seven hypotheses, and the first hypothesis tests for the impact on unemployment of EZs versus their surrounding communities, while the remaining hypotheses test for differences between EZs. The result of the first hypothesis is the foundation of the national study. The results of the remaining hypotheses describe the impacts of variables between the EZs. Chapter VI provides a predictive model of EZs, and discusses the major policy implications and recommendations resulting from the national study.

Part Two is comprised of Chapter VII only. Chapter VII discusses the contextual elements of the Portland EZ, reviews the data results of the single case study, and describes policy implications and recommendations. Let me state again that the first two chapters of Part One also form the intellectual building blocks for Part Two. Thus, Part One has chapters that support both studies. Also, comparisons and references are made between the two studies throughout Part One.

RESULTS

The following description of the results is to provide the reader with a summary of the two studies. Thus, the overall Preface is more in line with a research abstract or precis.

NATIONAL STUDY

The results of the national study (Part One) show that the impact of EZs on decreasing the unemployment rates of zone residents is _significant._ Also, the interventionist factors of length of time since designation, type of incentives, and number of incentives are all *significant* indicators of different performances between EZs. The employer-based incentives of property tax abatements and income tax credits are the types of incentives in the states that are *significant*. However, the descriptive factors of land use, population, and geographic size are not significantly influential.

SINGLE CASE STUDY

The results of the single case study (Part Two) show that a *majority* of new hires in the participating businesses in Portland are zone residents.

POLICY IMPLICATIONS AND RECOMMENDATIONS

NATIONAL STUDY

The major policy implications and recommendations from the national study (Part One) are:

1. That a full-scale incentives package with employer-based property tax abatements and income tax credits, along with other incentives, should be implemented by all state EZ programs, which would reduce unemployment.

2. That additional economic incentives, and especially investor-based capital gains tax exclusions along with financial incentives and reducing regulations, should be enacted by amending the federal Empowerment Zone program, which would enhance the state EZ programs and reduce unemployment.

3. That additional targeted and economically depressed areas should be designated as EZs and provided with substantive economic incentives by amending the federal Empowerment Zone program (and not merely designating dozens and dozens of communities for meager provisions), which would reduce unemployment.

4. That annual unemployment rate reports on EZs and their surrounding

communities should be mandated by the federal and state governments, which would enhance further evaluation of the outcomes of EZs.

SINGLE CASE STUDY

The major policy implications and recommendations from the single case study (Part Two) are:

1. That additional economic incentives should be provided by the State of Oregon, such as combining employer-based income tax credits with the existing property tax abatements, which would increase the number of participating businesses and the hiring of zone residents.

2. That specific data be mandated and derived on new hires, zone residents, and participating businesses for all state and federal EZ programs, which would enhance further evaluation of the outcomes of EZs.

3. That a formal job referral and training provider network, which is largely constituted of private organizations, should be provided at the local level for all state and federal EZ programs.

SUMMARY STATEMENT

In sum, these two studies show that EZs do have a major and significant impact on increasing employment for zone residents.

Terry Wm. Van Allen

PART ONE

A NATIONAL STUDY AND SCOPE

CHAPTER I

BACKGROUND DEVELOPMENT AND THE RESEARCH PROBLEM

HISTORICAL CONTEXT

The Enterprise Zone (EZ) is a public-private cooperative policy tool with an emphasis on free market principles for targeting economic development incentives into specific geographical areas suffering from economic distress or depression. Job creation and retention are primary goals of an EZ program, along with greater entrepreneurship opportunities for zone residents, and community improvements, such as redeveloping neighborhoods and business districts, improving the infrastructure, and improving the safety and welfare of local residents.

GREAT BRITAIN AND THE UNITED STATES

EZs were officially conceptualized as formidable public policy, instead of merely academic theory, in a 1978 speech delivered in London's depressed dockland district by Sir Geoffrey Howe, member of Great Britain's House of Commons, who later became Chancellor of the Exchequer (equivalent to a Treasury Secretary) and then Foreign Secretary in Margaret Thatcher's Conservative government. Howe had taken the framework for EZs primarily from Peter Hall, Ph.D., a British urban planning expert from Reading University and former chairman of the Fabian Society, based upon Hall's analysis of the free port (no tariffs) and economic activity of the British governed city-state of Hong Kong, with the idea of creating mini-Hong Kongs within Britain's inner cities (S. Butler 1980, 1981, 1991; Hall 1991).

Howe's elaboration of the EZ concept came directly after Sir Keith Joseph, another leading Conservative politician, announced at a conference arranged by the Adam Smith Institute that when elected the next Conservative government would establish a number of "demonstration zones." Eventually, Britain adopted and adapted its colony's economic growth model in selected industrial areas by passing EZ legislation under Mrs. Thatcher's leadership as the Prime Minister. Britain's designated zones were chiefly non-residential areas (Hall 1991). Elsewhere, variations of Hong Kongs' enterprise development activities have been utilized as Export Processing Zones (EPZs) in many Third World countries, that is to a large extent in East Asia and to a small extent in Latin America (Grunwald 1991).

The concept has evolved in America to provide primarily tax and financial incentives, along with regulatory relief, to various economically depressed and distressed areas in both urban and rural communities. Each EZ program is to serve as an experimental or pilot program of targeted economic development and entrepreneurship in forming a model for any others to adopt. The underlying feature in Hall's analysis is that government had either incrementally caused or exacerbated urban blight by creating barriers (most notably tax burdens, plus prohibitive regulatory and planning policies) to hinder the creation, retention, and expansion of business, thereby resulting in increased unemployment. However unconscious in intent, business districts and neighborhoods have declined, and population shifts have accelerated due in part to governmental policies, thus causing shrinking tax bases and swelling social problems.

There may be other societal causes than deleterious governmental policies that contribute to urban blight. But government can elect to remove any unnecessary barriers, such as heavy tax burdens, that it has contributed to poverty, unemployment, and especially, the urban flight of businesses and working/taxpaying residents (Moore and Stansel 1993; Sennholz 1987). That is why EZs have been conceived and widely applauded (and widely criticized) as a grand experiment to remove governmental barriers, and thereby creating a "stimulus" to economic activity and the reduction of unemployment. Rural areas have been included in state legislation as well as the more evident needs in urban areas. In large part, EZs are a new initiative brought about by the massive failure of previous governmental programs in using large bureaucracies with massive spending and anti-market place planning to respond effectively to community blight (S. Butler 1980, 1981, 1991; Hall 1991).

Subsequently after being conceived and proposed in Britain, conservative Congressman Jack Kemp from New York developed an expanded American version of the EZ concept after studying an income tax incentive program that positively affects Puerto Rico's industries and after reviewing an edifying EZ position paper by The Heritage Foundation's Stuart Butler, Ph.D., which summarized Howe's proposal. Kemp led the charge and introduced a highly substantive EZ bill in congress (S. Butler 1980, 1981, 1991). Liberal Congressman Robert Garcia, representing the decayed and blighted South Bronx of New York, endorsed this concept and co-sponsored a new EZ bill with Kemp, and Liberal Congressman Charles Rangel, representing another well-renown slum area in New York's Harlem district, provided additional support. The 1981 Kemp-Garcia Enterprise Zone bill (H.R. 7563) came onto the scene with both liberals and conservatives providing support (S. Butler 1981, 1991; Wolf 1989a).

Along with a bipartisan coalition in congress, additional support came from the Reagan Administration and other significant organizations, such as the Congressional Black Caucus, the National Urban League, the National Association for the Advancement of Colored People, and the National League of Cities (S. Butler 1991). Much of the support in establishing EZs has come from state and federal legislators who are minorities, since there are large concentrations of minorities in impoverished areas. Two important points for EZ support by minorities are (1) that small business minority entrepreneurs tend to hire minority employees (Bates 1993); and (2) that minority communities with strong minority-owned small business activities have produced residents who have higher rates of college graduates, professionals, entrepreneurs, and incomes than minority communities with weak minority-owned small business activities. In fact, minority entrepreneurs provide community leadership with support for education, recreation, crime control, and all functions of a stable and prosperous community (J. Butler 1991; Woodson 1987).

Both British and American liberals were disappointed in the poor results of massive governmental expenditures, such as British and American versions of Urban

Renewal and Model Cities programs that only displaced many of the poor (Butler 1981; M. and R. Friedman 1979; Rothenberg 1967), thus many liberals were attracted to a new governmental initiative to help the needy. Both British and American conservatives were attracted to limiting governmental spending programs and to stimulating the free market opportunities within impoverished areas (S. Butler 1981, 1991). There was a growing sentiment that EZ incentives are a "tool," and this tool was a way to have incremental and efficacious impact on reversing economic blight (Pierce 1986; Wolf 1989a, 1990).

¥ Battles over turf by the U.S. Departments of Treasury, Commerce, and Housing and Urban Development (Mellor 1987), along with resistance by key legislative and executive officials (S. Butler 1991; Mellor 1987), had stalled the passing of any federal legislation until 1987 with the passage of Title VII (Enterprise Zone Development) of the Housing and Community Development Act [Public Law 100-242]. However, this was merely a "symbolic" bill, in which the U.S. Department of Housing and Urban Development (HUD) was deemed the appropriate agency to administer the program (Wolf 1989). During 1988 another short delay occurred before implementation, when administrative rules had to be ironed out. This legislation authorized the Secretary of HUD to designate 100 severely distressed EZs across the nation. Yet, the legislation lacked any tax and financial incentives, therefore it has lacked any significant impact (Erickson and Friedman 1991).

Differing views on any revenue losses that might occur by implementing "substantive" federal legislation also significantly slowed the process (Butler 1983; Kemp 1984), and this debate has slowed any progress until recently, when the overwhelming need for a substantive federal EZ program became more apparent in the aftermath of the 1992 urban riots. Jack Kemp (1984) has strongly argued that there cannot be significant revenue loss by providing incentives to where there is no or little revenue production to begin with, and only revenue gain can result from broadening the tax base by increasing jobs with greater capital gains and profits, where there currently are few or none. Part of something (by stimulating production with tax rate cuts) is better than all of nothing (by prohibiting production with high tax rate barriers). In fact, another budgetary benefit of increased economic activity and employment in EZs would be lower levels of public welfare expenditures and less public dependency for local residents.

Rightly or wrongly, a perception of EZs resulting in significant revenue losses and incentive costs prevailed by the leaders in congress during the 1980s, however laudable the EZ goals of economic development. In light of the across-the-board 1981 Kemp-Roth tax cut, the 1981-82 recession (induced by previous inflation), large deficit spending, federalism, deregulation, sustained economic growth evidenced by numerous positive indicators (i.e., an increasing gross domestic/national product, a decreasing inflation rate, a decreasing interest rate, a decreasing poverty rate, and a decreasing unemployment rate) after 1982 and throughout the remaining decade, and ideological embattled congressional and executive branches, there seemed to be no legislative will in the 1980s to add a targeted incentive program to the plate by pushing federal EZs forward.

Additionally, the 1986 Tax Reform Act decelerated momentum for any meaningful EZ legislation, since a "tax neutral" position headed by President Ronald Reagan on the new tax codes dominated the reform. Without a tax neutral position, there was little possibility for the greatly needed tax reform, which was the Reagan Administration's priority. Many tax loopholes for higher income levels were removed, rates were lowered, and there was no political will to add tax incentives for anyone, including the blighted communities (S. Butler 1991). Although, Reagan did get congress to pass symbolic EZ legislation (as noted earlier) with the hope of *future* amendments adding economic incentives to the federal program.

Substantive federal EZs appeared to be a good idea, whose time had not yet come. Ultimately, it has taken over a decade, since a federal bill was first conceived and proposed by Jack Kemp, for advocates of federal EZ legislation to finally gain the momentum to raise EZs into one of the more important urban and economic redevelopment issues in America.

STATE PROGRAMS

Contrary to the federal legislative logjam, legislation at the state level exploded in the 1980s. There were 37 states and the District of Columbia that formed some kind of EZ legislation in the 1980s, plus Nebraska was added to the list with 1992 legislation, which makes a total of 38 states mandating over 3,000 EZ areas with each state providing its own variety of state and local incentives. A listing of the states and number of zones is given in Appendix A (U.S. Housing and Urban Development 1992). California has legislated two distinct state programs. Quite different from the other states, Mississippi and South Carolina have general rather than targeted EZ legislation, and Maine has subsidized grants rather than tax and financial incentives (Erickson and Friedman 1991).

Currently, Maine, Minnesota and Mississippi ended their EZ programs with sunset provisions. However these states are expected to renew their EZ mandates. New EZ programs have been proposed in many of the remaining 12 states without current or previous legislation, so there could be a few more states with programs in the near future. New, broad, and meaningful federal legislation could spur on new state programs, as more and more states would want to be included in receiving federal incentives for their programs.

The statements of intent in state legislation or administrative descriptions show that the majority of EZ programs specifically cite job creation as the most commonly stated priority. Specific references to health, safety, and welfare (as a group of goals) are the next highest stated priority and are included in the statements of intent by slightly less than half of the states. General statements of intent on neighborhood revitalization, community development, and public-private collaboration are included in some, but not in the majority of the states (Friedman and Erickson 1991).

The EZ programs for each of the states are as varied as the states themselves, which is seen as a positive to the subscribers of the experimental model approach of EZs (Verstandig 1985). The states tend to have varied tax and financial incentive packages. The most common incentives tend to be tax incentives, which include local property tax abatements, state and local sales tax waivers, state and local income tax credits for employers and/or employees, and state investment tax credits. Targeted areas sometimes have financial provisions for state sponsored loans and/or for industrial development bonds (IDBs). Although strongly advocated in the original concept, the proposals for local regulatory relief, such as the waiving of prohibitive local building and zoning laws, administrative procedures and red tape, and licensing and fees, have never been widely implemented with any tenacity (Erickson and Friedman 1991; U.S. Department of Housing and Urban Development 1988; Wolf 1990).

State programs are widely varied in the number of designation criteria, number of designated zones, and number of incentives. Several states literally have hundreds of EZs that have been designated in multitudinous rural and urban areas. Generally speaking, states with between 5-75 designated zones and with greater incentive packages tend to have better success at economic development due to their highly concentrated efforts. Those states with fewer than 5 designated zones tend to have limited incentives and symbolic legislation. States with a greater number of designation criteria (in qualifying for zone status) tend to have a greater number of incentives, which manifests a greater emphasis on the programs by the state legislatures. Thus, the state legislatures that give the most thought and care to a quality EZ program tend to have more criteria to qualify for designation to limit the number of zones and more incentives (both in quality and quantity) to give a concentrated effort to increase economic activity (Erickson and Friedman 1991; Erickson and Friedman and McCluskey 1989).

In an effort to be in line for future federal designation, many states have written their bills with designation criteria that would be similar to potential federal guidelines (Wolf 1989). Most notably, the criteria conformed in the urban arena to Urban Development Action Grant (UDAG) guidelines administered by HUD, which provides a formula based mainly on unemployment rates, poverty rates, and population losses (Business Facilities 1988; Kemp 1984; U.S. Department of Housing and Urban Development 1988).

It is interesting to note in the United States that much of the West has been slow to enact EZ legislation, although the Midwest and Southwest do have numerous states with programs. Oregon is the only state in the Pacific Northwest to currently have EZ legislation. Most of the states mandating EZ programs are in the country's other regions. Many of these regions have experienced historical declines in labor for industry and manufacturing, affecting large segments of their populations, which have resulted in increased poverty, unemployment, and population shifts (S. Butler 1980, 1981; Erickson and Friedman 1991). This economic decline in many localities within these regions has fostered EZ programs.

SMALL BUSINESS

Small business is generally defined as any business with the number of employees ranging between 1-100 and up to 500 when including medium-size business (U.S. Congress 1992). Thus, the categorical description of small business actually refers to "small-to-medium business" versus large-size business.

Since the vast majority of new jobs are created at the small business level (S. Butler, 1991), since the vast majority of entry and low skilled jobs are created at the small business level (S. Butler 1980, 1981), since old buildings provide lower costs in space for a wide variety of small businesses (Jacobs 1961), and since zone residents can become employers as well as employees more easily in a small business environment (Kemp 1984), state EZ legislation has often targeted incentives at small business development. Although, all EZ programs in all states tend to vigorously welcome major corporations. For the most part, taxes are far greater concerns to small firms and their survival than to large corporations (Armey 1992; S. Butler 1981; U.S. Congress 1992), although tax incentives can greatly enhance any size of business--small, medium, or large.

Yet, capital is a primary concern of both start-up and expanding businesses. Some argue that capital and finance incentives for the first few years of a small business venture are frequently more attractive than deductible income tax incentives, since a profit is very often not made in the first few years of a new small firm (S. Butler 1982a).

Conversely, all businesses pay significant property taxes in the form of property construction and ownership, or in lease and rental costs. Small businesses tend to contract for leases, which include property tax assessments in the prices required by owners who lease or rent out their buildings and properties. Sales taxes for many small businesses are also significant in the first and subsequent years of a new or expanding enterprise.

Many states opt for an incentive or a package of incentives that include small businesses across-the-board (commercial, retail and service along with manufacturing, technological and industrial sectors), but some states focus on incentives for one type of business (such as manufacturing) as is done for the industrial parks of Great Britain.   When the industrial sector is targeted by the state EZ programs, then legislation tends to provide incentives for medium and large-size businesses, as is the case in Oregon.   For instance, in contrast to the great emphasis on small business by many states, Oregon EZ legislation has restrictive incentives and does not target small business, even though passage of legislation was lobbied by small business associations, so medium and large-size companies have been the ones to chiefly (but not exclusively) benefit from Oregon's EZ programs.

PROPOSED FEDERAL INCENTIVES

In the past, substantive federal tax and financial incentives have been proposed to be combined with state incentives, but major federal incentives have never become law, which will be discussed later.   Major incentives at the federal level that have been proposed are substantive capital gains tax reductions, investment tax credits, expensing waivers on stock purchases, and loan interest deductions.   Other proposed incentives are substantive federal income tax credits for employers and employees. Between the various types of federal tax incentives, those that stimulate capital gains and capital formation for employers are viewed as the most substantial for creating jobs.   It does not have quite as much impact to give a tax credit to prospective employees if there are no or few job opportunities available to utilize the incentive. Also, weak incentives and those incentives with onerous regulatory stipulations for employers are viewed to have little impact on employment.

Several proposed packages of federal legislation have had a stronger emphasis in the targeting of individuals (jobless) and groups (zone residents) through economic incentives than most of the states.   Federal income tax incentives have been proposed for both employers and new employees--for employers hiring zone residents with an additional credit for hiring the unemployed, and for new employees who are zone residents with an additional credit if they were unemployed. Since federal income tax rates are larger than state and local income taxes, zone residents and the unemployed can be better targeted with the larger federal income tax incentives.

Other proposed federal EZ incentives for individuals or groups have included social security tax credits for employees who were unemployed and for employers hiring new employees who were unemployed. Federal welfare and health insurance provisions have been proposed to be gradually or decrementally fazed out for new employees, instead of new employees being immediately being cut off from public health care assistance upon employment. Federal child day care credits have been proposed for working parents. Finally, expanded federal job training credits have also been proposed, as many employers find job training programs very attractive (Butler 1982b; National Association of State Development Agencies 1985). An example of addressing the need for this last type of program is the North/Northeast Portland, Oregon EZ program, which is a model for utilizing a very large job referral and job training provider network (JOB-NET), including the federal Job Training Partnership Act (JTPA) program as a small component of the network (see Part Two, Chapter VII).

SOCIAL AND BUSINESS GOALS

State and local EZ incentives have been aimed more at stimulating business and economic activity with the by-product resulting in serving many social needs, especially in the hiring of unemployed EZ residents. Some critics have declared a dichotomy between social and business interests. However, state programs have tended to blend the two, and have used business goals as the starting-point, due to the types of economic incentives available, and social goals as the by-product.

Most of the state programs have incentives for businesses, while a few state programs have incentives for individuals and groups (unemployed zone residents). Due to the social philosophy and kinds of incentives available at the federal level, the targeting of individuals and groups have been given more emphasis in proposed federal legislation.

Whether social needs are inherently met as a by-product of targeting business and economic growth, or economic incentives are merely used as the means to target specific social ends, both business and social impacts are goals of EZs (Kemp 1984). In light of the recent urban riots, jobs and economic growth have been increasingly seen as a great social need, thus "blending" business and social needs.

Among other things that will commented upon in Chapter II, the recent urban riots brought into acute recognition that both the hope for and experience of having a job or working in a career or succeeding as an entrepreneur, is an essential part of an individual's fundamental social need in every community. Former HUD Secretary Kemp's axiom is that people *do not destroy* either (1) that which they own of value or (2) that in which they have an economic stake (Limbaugh 1992). Another common axiom is that the best social program is a good job. These are the fingerposts and postulates upon which people of widely diverse political views agree in their support of substantive federal EZ programs being implemented in blighted areas.

FEDERAL LEGISLATION IN THE 1990s

The future of meaningful federal EZ legislation looked promising at the end of the 1980s (Green 1990), and then into the early 1990s based upon several facts: (1) that the foremost advocate of EZs, Jack Kemp, has served as the Cabinet Secretary for HUD and has well-articulated a great need for EZs; (2) that resistance by key politicians has in fact been reversed to avid support (Congressman Daniel Rostenkowski, a long-tenured Democrat from Illinois who, at the time, was serving as chairman of the House's Ways and Means Committee, is a case in point); (3) that several years have passed since the last major tax (neutral) reform act; (4) that there have been numerous success stories by many state programs; (5) that there are perceived failures in previous governmental spending programs; and most importantly, (6) that there is a growing demand for federal support to combine with state and local programs due to the continued decay of a great many American cities.

This last point has been highlighted in the media coverage after the urban riots, especially those that occurred in South Central Los Angeles, in the spring of 1992. Ironically, part of the South Central Los Angeles rioted area already has a state EZ program, so this violent outburst of frustration and destruction has been a clarion call for a new and greater federal initiative to be combined with the various state programs.

In the early 1990s, Congressman Rostenkowski proposed a bill with incentives for a limited number (25) of federal EZs to support business creation and retention. Congressman Rangel proposed an expanded bill with incentives for a greater number (100) of federal EZs, plus he wanted to link in new and massive welfare services and public expenditures for EZs (Tucker 1991). Neither bill had the legislative support to pass on its own.

After the urban riots in the spring of 1992, and in the climate of ever-increasing blight in many urban and rural areas, along with ever-decreasing capital formation and investment in these areas, there was much support in both houses of congress for stimulating capital formation and investment through federally targeted EZs. Although capital incentives were more controversial than labor incentives for the U.S. Senate (U.S. Library of Congress 1992a), capital gains tax exclusions and investment credits on stock purchases were given the greatest emphases in policy formation by the U.S. House of Representatives and Bush Administration with the goal of unleashing venture capital provisions into these poverty areas (U.S. Library of Congress 1992b). Capital formation is the greatest concern of entrepreneurs and minority business owners (Green and Pryde 1989; Pryde 1987; *Wall Street Journal* 1993). In the fall of 1992, the House's version of an EZ bill was also passed by the Senate allowing for capital provisions, but it was the various amendments contained in the overall bill that caused an executive veto. EZs accounted for only 10% of the spending in the bill.

The most recent federal EZ legislation was passed as a watered down version during the summer of 1993, which provided very few economic incentives (in comparison to previous proposals) for designated "empowerment zones" in poor communities. There are to be a total of nine demonstration or empowerment zones (six urban and three rural), which will receive some limited income tax incentives. An additional 95 enterprise communities (65 urban and 30 rural) will be designated without any tax incentives. In addition, Indian Reservations were given some more welfare provisions in this bill.

The EZ package primarily has two provisions: (A) a small employer income tax credit (20% of the first $15,000 per new employee who is an empowerment zone resident until 2001, then 15% in 2002, 10% in 2003, and 5% in 2004) will be available for the nine zones; and (B) modest portions of tax-exempt facility bonds (maximums of $3,000,000 for any one zone or community, and $20,000,000 for all zones and communities) will be available for all designated areas.

The chief emphasis will be on expanding and streamlining block grant and welfare programs with more federal versus local control, rather than on financial and tax incentives for local initiatives and enterprises in indigent areas. All of the empowerment zones and enterprise communities will be regulated through a federal Enterprise Board. This centrally-managed program has an implementation time-table of 1994-95.

While Governor of Arkansas, President William Clinton enacted state EZ legislation and now he has enacted federal EZ provisions, however modest, in this recent legislation by the U.S. congress. He was able to get his overall legislative package passed, but with enormous political arm-twisting due to the major tax increases and budgetary spending imbalances in the overall bill. The bill passed by a single vote in each house of congress.

In addition to the empowerment zones and enterprise communities, there were two narrow provisions relating to economic development, which were included in this bill and can be applied to the zones and communities, as well as to all other areas. These are: (A) capital gains tax exemptions at 50% for long term (5 years or more) holdings on start-up businesses owned by minorities or the disadvantaged (but only industrial or manufacturing businesses are eligible), and (B) capital investment tax credits for small businesses on the first $17,500 of new equipment acquisitions.

Clinton declared in principle during his first State of the Union Address to the U.S. Congress that there should be community development banks in EZ areas. Additionally, the House has passed a bill to provide funds through existing commercial lenders, while the Senate has passed a bill to charter new single-mission lenders. A negotiated agreement between both houses should be forthcoming in the near future and it would represent another modest step toward eventually providing meaningful and effective federal EZs.

In contrast to specific empowerment zones, it should be noted that the Clinton Administration had previously proposed raising tax rates and cutting tax incentives provided in Section 936 of the commonwealth laws. A compromise policy was passed by congress, which retained much, but not all, of the tax provisions. Ironically, the Clinton proposal could have reversed much of the economic development for the indigent people of Puerto Rico by eliminating or curtailing the incentives to American corporations, which made the island the technological powerhouse of the Caribbean. However, the Governor of Puerto Rico could implement new incentives for native companies, especially for small businesses, which are excessively taxed with ten times the capital gains corporate rate in comparison to the large companies under Section 936. The important point is that the unique provisions of Section 936 fall under a very broad definition of an EZ program and are the key factor in the commonwealth's economic development (Daubon and Villamil 1991). Although, many of those who seek to eliminate the tax provisions, instead support statehood and full federal programs for Puerto Rico.

In sum, it still may take several more years before substantive and expansive EZ legislation is passed at the federal level. The new legislation should forestall any passage of a substantive and expansive EZ program in the near future, while this modest program is implemented and evaluated in the next few years. However, the underlying momentum to better address poverty issues in urban and rural areas through large-scale economic empowerment, slowly and continuously gains in strength. Continuous bipartisan support, ever-mounting and severe urban crises, and renewed debates in future congressional and presidential elections could again raise the issue of substantive and expansive (versus meager) EZs to heightened national attention. It is foreseeable that an evolutionary move beyond meager demonstration zones to a substantive and expansive federal EZ program could result later in the 1990s with new presidential leadership.

RESEARCH OBJECTIVES

PURPOSE OF THE STUDY

The purpose of this study is to evaluate the impacts of state Enterprise Zones on unemployment throughout the nation. There appears to be few studies on the "results" of EZs (Green 1990). Since 1985, the May issue of *Business Facilities* magazine has provided a "feature" on updated results on the growing number of jobs, businesses, and investment dollars in EZs. HUD published a "ten case studies" report in 1986, which also gave positive reviews on the fiscal impacts (U.S. Department of Housing and Urban Development 1986). But this national study in Part One goes beyond previous fiscal impact studies, and it contributes a quality national analysis on the unemployment impacts of EZs. The single case study in Part Two was added to provide another step forward in researching employment outcomes by analyzing specific job hiring impacts in the North/Northeast Portland, Oregon EZ program.

Most of the literature is a theoretical discussion on these two issues: (1) why or why not there should be EZs, and (2) what incentives should or should not be provided for EZs. Very little of the literature provides research on either the outcomes of EZs or what causes these outcomes. This appears to be due to the fact that EZs were conceived in this country only a decade and a half ago, and that most of the debate has been in the justification for the creating or preventing of them. There is a big gap in the literature on EZ employment outcomes and explanations for these outcomes within the context of varying EZ incentives and programs.

Most studies within the states have been on fiscal impacts and there has been only one other "national" study on EZs in the academic literature, and this was by Rodney A. Erickson and Susan W. Friedman (along with Richard E. McCluskey) of Pennsylvania State University (1989), which will be discussed again in the Literature Review section of the next chapter. But their study did not evaluate any EZ employment impact specifically on zone residents, and the data gathered in 1985-86 on EZ programs by HUD (which was used in their study) was limited since most EZs existed for only a few years, thus restricting any time series analysis.

This study is the *first* national study on EZs ever to focus on "unemployment impacts on zone residents over a period of time." Additionally, the single case study in Part Two is the *first* case study on an EZ ever to focus on "employment outcomes with actual numbers of jobs created versus actual numbers of zone residents hired." This national study along with the supplemental case study will provide important analyses on the area of EZ employment where there is a large gap in the published findings. This research will hopefully make a significant contribution to the field of knowledge, since EZs are still relatively new and the emergence of data based on results is becoming increasingly possible to collect. This work will also serve as a formal report to the U.S. Department of Housing and Urban Development.

In sum, this research will have more data collected on EZ impacts for evaluation than earlier studies. It has a supplemental case study of critical significance, and it focuses on important analyses for EZs, which are, unemployment impacts and employment outcomes.

LIST OF ACCOMPLISHED OBJECTIVES

The following is a list of the six major research objectives that this national study accomplishes:

1. It is only the second national social science research study on EZs with a broad scope of national significance having a cross-section of many states (and their localities) in many regions, and it is the first to include locational differences between the EZs.

2. It has an analysis on unemployment rates in regard to zone residents and the surrounding communities, which has never before been researched within a national scope.

3. It is the first study having the benefit of providing data results based on many years throughout the 1980s, instead of a very short time frame as other studies have used, which gives this infant field of research more substantial information for evaluation and increased understanding.

4. It is one of only a handful of academic research studies on EZs, and is results-oriented in evaluating EZ impacts, thus giving public policy formulation more scientific input, which lifts the debate above merely philosophical, speculative, ideological, and political deliberation.

5. It contributes much needed research findings at a time when EZs are a significant public policy issue at the federal level.

6. It adds a supplemental section that takes a crucial step forward with greater precision in defining specific employment outcomes for zone and local residents with a case study analysis.

SCHOLARLY INPUT

The author has discussed this study with seven highly respected EZ researchers. These are: Stuart Butler, Ph.D. (The Heritage Foundation), Michael Brintnall, Ph.D. (American Political Science Association), Rodney Erickson, Ph.D. (Pennsylvania State University), Roy Green (U.S. General Accounting Office), Marilyn Marks Rubin, Ph.D. (City University of New York), and Michael Wolf, Ph.D. (University of Richmond).

All have unanimously stated that this national study in Part One and the supplemental single case study in Part Two make major contributions to the field, especially in discovering EZ outcomes and in pointing out what EZ elements need to be researched further. The debate is extremely vicious between proponents and opponents as well as between factious proponents of EZs, especially on the specific benefits to zone residents. It is for this reason and for the fact that the national study has some measurement imprecisions in regard to unemployment rates, that the author is providing a supplemental section on an essential element of a case study in Part Two, which presents detailed information on employment for "zone residents" in North/Northeast Portland, Oregon. While the national study lends itself to a more sophisticated statistical methodology in analyzing general employment outcomes, the supplemental case study provides an advanced step in the detailed analysis of zone residents and employment outcomes for a specific EZ. The author resided in

Portland, Oregon while investigating and authoring these two studies, which makes the findings of the supplemental single case study in Part Two to be of particular interest to him.

CHAPTER II

THE CONCEPTUAL FRAMEWORK

ECONOMIC THEORIES

There are three main components of economic theories which are the foundation of EZs and increasing employment. These theories and components are (1) microeconomic theory, with an emphasis on production costs and prices, as well as capital financing and budgeting (price theory and managerial economic theory are major subcomponents of microeconomics); (2) supply-side economic theory, with an emphasis on stimulating economic growth through fiscal policy incentives for production (while stimulating consumption, which is the demand-side, as a by-product of increased production); and (3) urban economic theory, with an emphasis on location, choice, mobility, and community (which also applies to rural areas). Some components of these three theories will overlap.

MICROECONOMICS

The first theory, microeconomics, has elements based upon the firm's costs of production, optimal prices, marginal profits, capital assets, and the demand of the product (Mansfield 1990; Nicholson 1992; Watson 1991). Lower production costs cause lower prices, lower prices cause greater demand, and greater demand causes greater production, including increased labor. Also, greater productivity and lower prices create greater profit margins, and greater profit margins cause business creation, expansion, and retention, which positively impact the demand for labor.

The costs of production within "general price theory" may include costs from four general categories: (1) taxes, licensing, and fees; (2) property construction, expansion, renovation, purchasing or leasing; (3) equipment, inventory, operating expenses, and miscellaneous overhead expenses; and (4) the price and productivity of labor. This is compared to the prices of goods sold or services rendered, which determine profits. Assets (including profit and all forms of capital) and liabilities (including taxes, fees, and regulatory burdens with production costs) are the bottom line factors in the "managerial economic decision-making" of prices and production (including labor), and in the creation, expansion, and longevity of business ventures.

Taxes are an important factor for business (especially small and medium-size firms) in determining the prices of products and marginal profits, and ultimately in determining the creation and retention of jobs (S. Butler 1981). Property taxes tend to be a substantial amount of tax liability for businesses, but other state sales and income taxes (along with federal income taxes) play a substantial role in tax liability and the costs of doing business. Property taxes reflected in property ownership or leasing costs are especially evident as a liability for new small businesses, as they cut across all types of businesses. Sales taxes apply chiefly to retail, although equipment and supply purchases of manufacturing can play a role in this area. Income taxes apply to businesses and entrepreneurial occupations that make a profit, which often does not occur in the first few years of a newly created or expanded small business venture. Capital gains taxes apply to investment for all firms. With the exception of capital gains taxes, large businesses tend to not place as much emphasis on tax structures as do small businesses, due to other issues playing major roles in gaining access to larger and more distant markets. However, large high technology firms have tended to place the local and state tax structures as a higher priority than other large firms.

Microeconomic theory includes capital as an essential factor to business creation, expansion, and retention. The reduction of the costs of capital financing allows for venture capitalists to invest in and unleash capital into businesses. It also allows for employers and managers to make better economic decisions and to gain greater profits. The present cost and future return of capital budgeting cannot be overlooked and is a major factor in the development and success of any business.

In sum, decreasing the costs of production and capital increases the opportunity for greater production at the optimum price. This will lead to increased production and labor, although some increased productivity can occur through investing the cost savings in improved technology. Therefore, increased employment is a distinct result of the decreased costs of production, as well as a result of decreased costs in capital financing and budgeting. The purpose of EZs is to target a mandate for increasing the firm's rate of return and marginal price by decreasing the costs of production and capital, in highly unproductive localities, which will be an incentive for the increase in production and employment.

SUPPLY-SIDE ECONOMICS

The second theory, supply-side economics, is based upon increasing the incentives for production and capital (formation and earnings), which will stimulate economic growth, and is primarily accomplished through fiscal and tax policy (Roberts 1983; Wanniski 1989). (Supply-side economics also emphasizes a stable monetary policy based on an international commodity-price standard.) The fiscal emphasis is on entrepreneurship and productivity whereby greater production and investment are rewarded with greater profit, since the costs of both production and capital are reduced and the profit margin increased when tax rates are reduced. By reducing the costs for production and capital, there is an incentive for greater productivity and investment for the firm. This combined production and capital (formation and earnings) stimulus results in greater profits for the firm and greater employment for individuals. Additionally, a supply-side stimulus provides greater means and rewards for the development of new technologies and better products (goods and services) by the entrepreneur.

This production and capital (income gains) stimulus can also apply to an individual by reducing income and other taxes, and thereby increasing after-tax rewards and take home-pay, as an incentive for higher earnings and longer hours. This can also aid in increasing labor force participation (LFP) by making it more attractive to rise out from the welfare roll (Murray 1984).

In essence, a supply-side stimulus is based on the effects of the "marginal tax rate." In practice, this means that steeply ascending tax rates discourage productivity for the investor, employer, and employee, as additional dollars earned result in smaller percentages of after-tax rewards and take-home pay. Thus, lower and flatter tax rates encourage economic growth at both the micro and macro levels.

The costs of doing business include the costs that government places on free enterprise through taxes (and regulation). Governmental costs on both employer and employee are disincentives to production. Governmental costs reduce both employer and employee net incomes. Supply-side economists or supply-siders refer to this before-tax and after-tax equation as the "tax wedge." The supply-side modus is to reduce the governmental costs of the investor risking his capital, of the employer doing business, and of the employee performing work, which will increase productivity and the demand for increased labor. Therefore, the creation, expansion, and retention of businesses and their employees are influenced by the incentives and disincentives of production and profit.

Profit margins are substantially affected by taxes and regulations, especially for small-to-medium businesses. A recent study by the Joint Economic Committee of the U.S. Congress shows a direct, simultaneous, major, and inverse relationship between governmental burdens (taxes and regulations) and the profits of small-to-medium business (Armey 1992; U.S. Congress 1992). This congressional study shows clearly that--the greater are the governmental burdens, then the lesser are the profits for business, thus affecting productivity, labor, and employment. Another important and recent study (Vedder and Gallaway 1992, 1993) confirms this report and shows that regulations affecting wages and productivity costs have inversely, greatly, and historically impacted employment.

In the case of EZs, most of the supply-side incentives at the state level have been targeted toward business with a goal of job creation and retention. Although viewed with importance for rewarding individual initiative, tax incentives for individuals are not as effective if there are no jobs for unemployed or underemployed individuals to seek and obtain. Some of the most recent federal legislative proposals have followed this line of supply-side reasoning with the following prioritized capital and production incentives: (1) capital gains tax credits for investors or employers;

(2) stock investment credits for investors; (3) capital investment tax credits for employers; (4) income tax credits for employers; and lastly, (5) income tax credits for employees (Waltzman 1992).

THE LAFFER CURVE

A trade-off and comparison between tax rates and revenues constitute the foundation of supply-side theory on economic growth and government revenue. When illustrated as a slope on a graph (see Figure 1 on page 30), it is known as the "Laffer Curve" (conceived by Arthur B. Laffer). As you can see, a tax rate of 100% (with no incentive to invest, earn, and work, except in a black market economy) and a tax rate of 0% (with no public collection of income) will both produce "zero" tax revenue and an anarchic state. As the top rate of 100% drops, there is more and more incentive to invest, earn, and work; and on the other end, as the bottom rate of 0% rises, there is more tax revenue generated, that is, until the tax rate rises too high. When the tax rate rises too high, then there is less incentive to invest, earn, and work. Therefore, less tax revenue is generated than would be the case if the tax rate were lower (see points "A" and "C" in Figure 1). Supply-siders have described this economic growth policy as "revenue enhancing tax cuts."

With the exception of an optimal point, there is always a state of equipollence where both a higher tax rate (which causes decreased economic growth and a small tax base) and a lower tax rate (which causes increased economic growth and a larger tax base) will generate the "same" tax revenue on a long term basis (see points "A" and "B" in Figure 1). Thus, a public policy can attain the same level of government income, while promoting economic growth and prosperity in the private economy by reducing high tax rates.

The *optimal point* (see point "C" in Figure 1) is where a specific tax rate will produce the greatest *long term* tax revenue, but this specific tax rate cannot be either excessively high or low to do so. This optimal point is not necessarily fixed at the mid-point, but it is a "relative range" based upon human action and behavior. Experience shows it is a range, when including "total taxation" from all levels of government, that is *measurably, consistently, and well below the mid-point.*

FIGURE 1

THE LAFFER CURVE

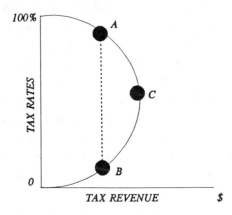

Overall, the basic premise of supply-side theory is that a lower tax rate will produce the same tax revenue as a higher tax rate, by stimulating more economic growth, employment and productivity, and therefore, a larger tax base and a healthier economy (with more production creating more consumption and savings). The reduction of excessive regulation also produces similar positive results as does the reduction of excessive taxation. Thus, reduced tax rates and regulations are much more desirable and beneficial to society. In sum, the "Laffer Curve" directly applies to the high policy goal of EZs to have maximal benefits at minimal costs.

PRODUCTION VERSUS CONSUMPTION POLICIES

Supply-side economics focusses on the "production" element of economic activity, whereas demand-side economics focusses on the "consumption" element of economic activity. Many governmental programs have focussed on the demand or consumption mode, with transfer or entitlement payments to welfare recipients, as well as grant funding for urban renewal. An increase in consumer spending actually means an increase in demand for products and services. To some degree, governmental programs have been formulated for consumption in an effort to stimulate more business activity and jobs, but have not proved satisfactory.

Since a more demand-side or consumption-driven model has been utilized in government programs from the 1960s to today, and since there has been a disappointing result amongst the minds of policy-makers with these programs, a supply-side or production-driven model is gaining in momentum and is being tried by over three-fourths of the states in the context of the EZ experiment. In sum, the *incentive* approach for stimulating production, including employment, is the basis of the supply-side theory, in which EZs are a microcosm for this model. This model is to stimulate business ownership as well as job creation and retention for zone residents.

Both sides of the economic equation are important, supply and demand, production and consumption. In a free market system, supply-side economic activity increases production, with the by-product resulting in increased jobs, business and home ownership, and overall consumption. Unfortunately, previous and current governmental programs have aided consumption without greatly impacting job creation and retention for the poor. Public social programs exist to redistribute consumption and do not have entrepreneurial incentives for greatly increasing production in impoverished areas.

Now, EZs are being established to directly provide incentives for greater production, which means greater job creation and retention for zone residents. Greater production in EZs and its multiplier effects will meet and increase the demand for the consumption of local goods and services. Greater production in EZs will aid in the stimulation of new opportunities of entrepreneurship, and business, property, and home ownership for zone residents in their communities.

URBAN ECONOMICS

The third theory, urban economics, has two primary components of spatial dimensions, one is based on distance and the other is based on non-distance (Hirsch 1984). This translates into location decisions for both producers and consumers. Some of the factors influencing business location decisions can be determined by applying microeconomic and supply-side economic principles to profit margins, prices, and the costs of production, which were discussed in the previous sections. Other factors influencing both production and consumption, such as consumer choice, access to markets, community identity and infrastructure, and crime, will be discussed in this section.

TIEBOUT HYPOTHESIS

There is a principle that differing or varying taxes between areas can have a major economic impact on business location, job location, and residential location based on "consumer choice." This means that having a lower tax in one community that is adjacent to a community with a higher tax, will result in greater demand by both communities for goods and/or services (due to lower prices) from the businesses in the lower tax community, than they normally would with equal taxation. This location theory is often described as "voting with one's feet" or the "Tiebout Hypothesis" (formulated by Charles Tiebout), where lower tax burdens are an attraction for consumers and producers, and has accounted for some of the urban flight (American Legislative Exchange Council 1993; Hirsch 1984; Moore and Stansel 1993; Price-Waterhouse 1992).

There are other nongovernmental factors involved in consumer choices, but this discussion centers on governmental factors. For example, residents in Vancouver, Washington (a high sales tax locality) will commute and purchase goods across the river in Portland Oregon (a no sales tax locality), with the results of increased retail business activity in Portland and decreased retail business activity in Vancouver. Due to the comparative advantage between tax systems, there are more retail businesses and jobs in Portland (per capita), and fewer retail businesses and jobs in Vancouver (per capita), even when comparing these localities to other cities (Vedder 1993).

Portland residents who commute and purchase goods in Vancouver are given a waiver of the sales tax, which serves as an incentive for retail business in Vancouver. But this does not offset the transportation and location advantage of retail business in Portland for its residents. Additionally, industrial businesses that make large purchases of equipment and supplies for production have an incentive to locate in Portland with no sales tax. Yet, other comparative advantages, such as differing property taxes, access to markets, and infrastructure, tend to influence the location of these businesses as well.

The location principle also applies to the residence and place of employment where thousands of employees reside in Vancouver, due to lower property taxes and housing costs, but work in the larger market place of Portland. In other words, this is job location versus residential location. These Washington residents must pay Oregon income taxes, yet they have a comparative advantage over their co-workers who commute to work and are Oregon residents, due to the difference in property taxes and housing costs.

Ironically, retail business has increased in Portland due to no sales taxes, while residential housing has increased in Vancouver due to lower property taxes. Due to the job location versus residential location, there is also a disparity in public revenue where Oregon income taxes are paid by Washington residents. In sum, this urban economic location theory of comparative tax advantages having significant influence on consumption and production applies to the EZ concept.

MOBILITY AND COMMUNITY

In regard to mobility and community, labor force mobility has always been a key ingredient to a healthy economy, but opportunity and access to job markets and high wages has been limited in blighted areas, both urban and rural, where the poor are concentrated (Sullivan 1990). There has been a debate between a "people to jobs" approach and a "jobs to people" approach (Hansen 1991). This latter approach is emphasized when a community and its cultural history are viewed as important values for community residents.   People have established histories and identities in communities, and the limitations of mobility and opportunity for indigent community residents compound the need to support the community, thus the inception of EZs (S. Butler 1981). A sound and mixed community has social, residential, educational, commercial, and industrial components in its identity (Jacobs 1961). The EZ program has been established to help meet the diverse needs of this urban economic reality.

There have been numerous articles written in the 1970s, and early 1980s, suggesting a public policy of urban "planned shrinkage" and "orderly disinvestment" and "planned abandonment" in an effort to facilitate the decreased economic activity in urban areas (S. Butler 1981). Some of these articles have even suggested that we should develop a European model for providing large-scale governmental subsidies for mobility, but a modified structure already exists in America. Federal income tax deductions already exist for moving expenses to new jobs and various polls cite that the average American moves to a new residence every 4-5 years. The enormous explosion of automobile ownership and moving van businesses, the existence of previously built roads and highways, the availability of air transportation, and the quick access of communication all contribute to a very mobile society. However, the urban poor have not been able to take full advantage of this impressive technology. The poor cannot afford moving expenses and do not have the job skills where their employment is highly demanded. Moreover, companies do not usually pay moving expenses for unskilled and entry level labor. So, for these reasons and for their established identities in communities, the urban poor have a great need for businesses, jobs, and entrepreneurial opportunities to be created and retained in their localities. This phenomenon of the lack of mobility also applies to the rural poor.

There is another urban economic or community development theory that public infrastructure and services can improve the economic plight of blighted areas (Mills 1987). For example, the building and maintaining of the transportation infrastructure (such as roads, bridges, and ports) can enhance the access to business markets for employers and to job markets for employees. Implementing better education and training programs, improving crime prevention with community policing, and expanding youth recreation programs are other examples that have been widely discussed in the media by politicians and political analysts, especially after the recent urban riots.

CRIME AND COMMUNITY DEVELOPMENT

The violence, pillaging, and destruction of the urban riots sent another message as well as one of perceived societal injustice. These disorderly, unlawful, and destructive acts illustrated the fact that high crime rates are great costs to local businesses and negatively affect local entrepreneurship and employment. High levels of crime drive out existing business and hinder new business, both directly and indirectly. Higher insurance premiums, more security costs, more inventory losses, more repair and maintenance costs, and less customer volume due to personal safety concerns, are examples of crime's negative affect on business. Crime-generated obstacles, along with the normal and high financial risks of any business venture, are strong disincentives to new businesses and frequently cause economic failure in existing businesses. Thus, governmental enforcement of justice, law, and order in the community is essential to economic opportunity and prosperity.

On one hand, there appears to be a direct relationship of crime causing or exacerbating economic decay in communities, and on the other hand, there seems to be marked exceptions to the thesis that poverty causes crime, with many anomalies in sociological and criminological studies and findings (Rubenstein 1992), such as low crime rates for the urban poor of Chinatown in the 1960s, the rural poor of West Virginia, *married* male adults in poor communities, and the Great Depression. But a central indicator of both crime and poverty in recent decades, especially for teenagers and children, is family stability versus family instability evidenced by "two-parent versus father-absent families" (Zinsmeister 1992).

Father-present families have fewer emotional and behavioral problems, fewer juvenile delinquents, fewer teenage pregnancies, fewer high school drop outs, fewer gang members, lower rates of drug abuse, lower rates of welfare dependency, and lower criminal rates for adults than father-absent families (Zinsmeister 1992). This may show an indirect relationship of poverty impacting crime and other social problems, since it is "joblessness," be it in the form of unemployment for job seekers (Wilson 1987) or especially in the form of labor force non-participation for non-job seekers due to welfare dependency, which contributes enormously to family instability and father-absent families Murray 1984). However, poverty's impact on family instability and crime is greatest when there is a lack of moral fiber in a culture or sub-culture (Davies 1992; Hertzel and Hughes 1987; Stack 1983). A lack of moral fiber in the form of illegitimacy is highly correlated with poverty and crime (Murray 1993). This chapter's primary emphasis on economics does not discount the importance of non-economic factors, such as moral and spiritual values to family stability, character building, constructive and productive citizenship, and lawful conduct. Non-economic factors will be discussed again later in this chapter.

Therefore, the most common attraction for establishing EZs and to produce more jobs and economic development, is the high goal of an improved community, i.e., greater family stability, greater neighborhood and business district tranquility, less governmental and welfare dependency, less crime perpetrated against citizens and local businesses, higher qualities of life, and greater economic empowerment for local residents. The ultimate attraction of EZs is the great need for an economic development program whereby communities can be incrementally revitalized and can be largely built from *within.*

In sum, the components of the aforesaid economic theories, involving (1) a firm's costs, prices, profits, labor, and capital, (2) supply-side or production stimuli through fiscal policy incentives, and (3) location decisions plus mobility and community factors, as the bases for utilizing economic principles for improving impoverished areas, lead to the fundamental point that EZs are a redevelopment program. Large-scale economic development in recent decades has occurred in suburbs and has fostered urban sprawl, due to economic opportunities and social realities. Thus, the EZ program's targeted goal is to "redevelop" blighted areas in inner cities and outer rural areas through economic revitalization, which will progressively "empower" local residents.

CRITICISMS

ZERO SUM ECONOMICS

Criticisms of zero sum economics naturally arise from a discussion on redevelopment and economic expansion. Zero sum economic theory and the redistributive division of an economic pie are not the primary building blocks of *pure* EZ theory, however much is said or done to the contrary. Many of the critics of EZs have an element of zero sum economic theory (where some individuals, groups, and businesses will be the winners at the expense of others, who as a consequence will be the losers) instead of a growing economic pie in their arguments. Those who do not trust business believe that targeted tax incentives will allow businesses to exploit the system and to make inequitable choices. While those who do not trust government believe that targeted tax incentives will allow politicians, bureaucrats, and special interest groups to cause inefficient and ineffectual choices.

Much of the zero sum criticism is rooted in a fear of a "donut effect" for businesses and individuals. For businesses, this means that those firms located directly outside will gain by relocating to inside of the zone, thus causing the zone businesses to lose out on customers while relocating businesses take over the market share. For individuals, this means that those individuals residing directly outside will be hired inside of the zone, thus causing the immediate surrounding residents to gain and the zone residents to lose out on jobs. But EZ theory proposes to (1) primarily create and expand businesses inside of the zone, and secondarily to attract the relocation of existing firms from outside of the zone; and (2) primarily create new jobs and entrepreneurial opportunities for individuals residing inside of the zone, and secondarily to serve as a job market for individuals residing outside of the zone. Thus, the direct benefits to EZ businesses and residents are primary, while the spillover effects for businesses and residents in the community at large are secondary.

In an empirical response to the concernes about benefits to businesses outside, and not inside, of the EZ, a previous EZ study by Elling and Sheldon (1991) on four midwestern states with 47 zones addressed the issue of business relocation. Elling and Sheldon found that for EZ activity (A) new businesses occurred between a 21-31% proportion, (B) expanding businesses occurred between a 55-66% proportion, and (C) *relocating* businesses occurred between a 7-16% proportion. Since business relocation is much lower than the other types of business growth activities, excessive relocation or zero sum activity appears to not be a legitimate policy fear in regard to EZs. (Although, states are tempted to compete for the location or relocation of medium-to-large businesses in their zones in an effort to create many jobs with quick swoops.) This important study by Elling and Sheldon will be cited again along with other noteworthy studies in the Literature Review section of this chapter.

In an empirical response to the concerns about benefits to those individuals outside, and not inside, of the EZ, this national research study and the supplemental single case study in Part Two address the question of employment for zone residents. The author's single case study in Part Two gives substantive evidence that the vast majority of new hires are zone residents.

Finally, it was high taxes and excessive regulations that helped to drive urban businesses away to outside areas in the first place as stated in Chapter I. At the least, the incentives provided by EZs would help to level the playing field in a zero sum game. Yet, the high goals of EZs are not to primarily attract relocating businesses, but to create and expand businesses inside of the zone as stated previously.

PREFERENTIAL TREATMENT AND BENEFIT-COST

The are many diverse criticisms espoused by opponents of EZs, but the common thread of many of these criticisms, is the perception of "preferential treatment" for things which these critics passionately oppose. These critics can be generally categorized into the following groups:

1. Critics who are pro-government (with socialist inclinations) and anti-business tend to perceive that certain businesses will be given preferential treatment, which they neither need nor deserve, and will exploit an EZ incentive policy for self-interest. These critics tend to believe that government should raise or maintain tax rates, and oppose the idea of utilizing tax incentives for any purposes, even economic growth. They believe that government and business are in a *polarized* conflict over resources and values in society.

2. Critics who are pro-business (with libertarian inclinations) and anti-government tend to perceive that government will pick winners and losers through redistribution schemes and the preferential treatment of special interest groups, which will do more overall harm to society than good. These critics tend to believe that imposed choices by government are inefficient and ineffectual, and are contrary to those that result *naturally* in a market system with free choice available to all citizens. Adding more public welfare supplements to EZ programs, which a few "big government" politicians have proposed, is also onerous to them. They also believe in a polarized conflict between business and government, especially due to the regulatory and redistributive policies of a governmental leviathan.

3. Critics who are both pro-government (with *big* government inclinations) and pro-business (with *big* business inclinations) tend to believe that individuals and groups (zone residents and small businesses) will receive preferential treatment, thus diluting the energies and abilities of major institutions, which are large-scale governmental programs and medium-to-large corporations, to be the chief corner-stones of economic growth. (In contrast, there are a few supporters of EZs, who would design EZ policy with these views in mind through major programs of targeted infrastructure rebuilding and targeted corporate incentives, as the only way to make a major impact on economic growth in targeted areas.)

4. Critics who focus mainly on costs can be aggregated together from all of the above, because, no matter of ideology, all critics tend to argue that the costs outweigh the benefits of EZs, even though most of these arguments rely on political reasoning or policy preferences rather than on empirical evidence. Some of these opponents cite the loss of public revenue and increase of the federal budget deficit, even if these claims are *not* supported by any proof. (Although, this modus of using selective rationalization rather than credible facts can apply to both sides of any issue, which makes the author's empirical studies most valuable.)

Previous sections have already addressed the issues raised by these critics. In a nutshell, EZs are a public-private cooperative policy tool that utilizes free market principles to target economic and social needs by creating jobs and entrepreneurial opportunities in blighted communities, which empower citizens to lead a productive life and to overcome a dependency on costly public programs. In this way, government and business become allies not enemies; free market incentives are utilized to stimulate economic growth and production and capital investment, while shunning zero sum win-lose community development schemes; the needy are provided with economic opportunities and can rise above welfare dependency; small entrepreneurial business is given the "green light" through incentives to continue to be the greatest entry level job creator in the country; and the tax base is broadened into areas where little tax revenue collection currently exists.

Additionally, in an empirical response to the benefit-cost criticism, a scholarly study by Marilyn Marks Rubin (1990, 1991), plus Rubin and Trawinski (1991), produced a benefit-cost analysis involving 976 Urban Enterprise Zone (UEZ) firms in New Jersey. Rubin found that EZs, with a modest multiplier effect, have a positive benefit-cost ratio of 1.9 to 1, or almost two to one for public revenues versus expenditures. Without any multiplier effect, EZs were still low in costs compared to other economic development programs. However, the conclusions of this important study by Rubin should be tempered due to methodological limitations, but it will be cited again, along with other noteworthy studies, in the Literature Review of this chapter.

NON-ECONOMIC FACTORS

EZs are based upon economic principles, but non-economic factors need to be included to help put economic factors into perspective. EZs have been mildly criticized by those who see them addressing only economic issues and point to the great need of improving values in morally debilitated communities, especially in the rearing of families. (The harsh debates by opponents and proponents on the merits and demerits of EZs are chiefly on economic issues as noted earlier.)

Virtuous values can influence or determine such things as family stability, honest character, good citizenship, personal and civic responsibility, and lawful and orderly conduct. Moral and spiritual values appear to be a common denominator for producing high levels of family stability and low levels of crime (Davies 1992; Hertel and Hughes 1987; Stack 1983), and for establishing economic well-being. Virtuous values can influence both the economic conditions and the work ethics of individuals, families, and communities. Notwithstanding the deleterious economic effects of cultural discrimination or personal limitation, the absence of moral and spiritual values can determine economic hardship, while the presence of moral spiritual values can determine the economic prosperity of individuals, families, and communities, which are the nuclei of a nation (Brookes 1982; Colson and Eckerd 1991; Freeman 1986; Lowry 1993; Reichley 1985).

On the flip side of the coin, economic prosperity can foster obsessive consumerism, hedonism, and materialism, which are also destructive to society (Davidson and Rees-Mogg 1991). Thus, one could argue that virtuous values are under attack when materialistic values, be they in the rich or poor, are the core of any standards of living.

Non-economic conditions are more qualitative and intangible than economic conditions. Their primal importance should not be overlooked, but for the most part, EZs deal chiefly with economic conditions in assisting blighted communities. Again, EZs are not a panacea, but are a powerful policy tool to assist in the economic empowerment of needy families, so that they will be better enabled to mould and elevate every aspect of their lives. Empowered families are the expression of productive individuals and are the nuclei of productive communities. Virtuous values have ascendancy over economic factors in the well-being of families, but economic empowerment can help stabilize families so that virtuous values will have a greater opportunity to flourish through wholesome home, church, school, recreational, and civic activities. Family stability is much more than an economic condition, but economic empowerment and economic freedom are fundamental in generating hope and fulfillment for families (Woodson, 1987).

ECONOMIC GOALS

A pure EZ policy is derived mainly upon the following seven goals of economic growth, which balance out most of the arguments against an EZ policy being implemented, by giving most policy-makers something to like about EZs:

1. EZs seek to eliminate governmental barriers to economic growth and to remove an adversarial relationship between government and business.

2. EZs seek to target communities and citizens in economic depression and distress.

3. EZs seek to utilize economic incentives to stimulate production through market principles instead of spending large amounts of governmental revenue on boondoggles and welfare dependency.

4. EZs seek to stimulate small to medium-size businesses where most of the new and entry level jobs, and entrepreneurial opportunities, are created.

5. EZs seek to stimulate economic growth and redevelopment from within, which will provide empowerment opportunities for zone residents within their neighborhoods and business communities.

6. EZs seek to improve the overall quality of life for residents by improving overall economic conditions for families and communities through jobs and

entrepreneurial opportunities.

7. EZs seek to broaden the tax base wide enough to produce greater benefits than costs, thus creating a win-win combination for private development and public finance.

There are gross variations of pure EZ theory where almost anything associated with economic development is called an EZ program. This does give the critics more ammunition to point out flaws and failures. But this can also serve as rallying point by advocates to illustrate the experimental nature of EZs where successful programs can be adopted elsewhere and unsuccessful programs can be used as lessons of what not to do.

In sum, the emotions of critics are very heated and strong due to their economic perceptions of zero sum winners and losers, preferential treatments, and costs versus benefits associated with EZs. Most of these arguments stem from political ideology, which is something deeper than the mere argumentation about the merits or demerits of EZs. The proponents of EZs seek to built a pluralistic coalition with those of diverse political views, if not a consensus, by formulating a policy that combines both business and social goals, and thereby cuts across the barriers of politics and ideology. Many policy-makers agree that there is a great need for EZs, and that EZs are a new policy developed from previous economic successes and failures, and that EZs may be the last available policy on economic redevelopment remaining to be tried at the federal level. Again, the recent urban riots have illustrated the crisis state of existence and public policy failures in blighted areas, which demand action by all policy-makers. This has given federal EZ policies, present and future, more momentum, as it usually takes an ongoing crisis, resulting from or exacerbated by past policy failures, for polarized parties to agree on a new policy initiative.

LITERATURE REVIEW

As noted earlier, there is much more to be learned about the results of EZs, as there have been only a small number of scholarly studies on EZs. The literature is dominated by discussions on the theoretical merits and demerits of EZs. This literature review will summarize the major writings on both the intellectual roots and the measured outcomes of EZs.

There are two books that stand out as authoritative works on EZs. These two books are actually the only books on EZs ever published in the United States. The first book by Stuart Butler (1981) gives a thorough theoretical analysis for the creation of EZs in the United States. Butler's ties to his native land, Great Britain, where the concept originally took hold as formidable public policy, enabled him to improve and develop an EZ concept for America through his policy analysis at a Washington-based think tank, The Heritage Foundation. In the late 1970s and early 1980s, Butler wrote position papers, conducted seminars, published articles, and authored the book *Enterprise Zones: Greenlining the Inner Cities*, all of which constituted the intellectual roots of EZs in America.

The major themes of Butler's analysis of economic rejuvenation and redevelopment in blighted communities are--providing tax and financial incentives, easing and removing regulatory barriers, and targeting small businesses where job growth and entrepreneurship have the greatest potential. After completing his monumental work on EZs, and with the passage of time and the emergence of other vital public policy issues, Butler has since formulated a new national health care policy, which, like his EZ analysis, is supported by many liberal and conservative policy analysts. However, Butler is still recognized as a leading EZ authority, as witnessed in an interview and policy debate published in a recent *Wall Street Journal* report on "Black Entrepreneurship" (February 19, 1993).

The second book is a collection of articles and studies published in 1991 by Sage Publications, entitled, *Enterprise Zones: New Directions in Economic Development*, and edited by Roy Green. The various chapters provide both policy discussions and research results. The intent of the book is to present scholarly contributions by the leading policy analysts and academic researchers. Since many of the writings on EZs have been done by politicians and journalists, and many of the studies on EZs have been general fiscal studies by state agencies without utilizing academic methodology, this book was intended to provide a single scholarly resource distinct from the plethora of non-academic writings on the subject of EZs. Thus, a well-reasoned and well-researched resource became available to new students of public policy in the field of EZs. The book was not intended to be exhaustive, but it was meant to highlight the leading academic thinking and findings on this particular subject. In sum, the most significant EZ research studies and analyses published or reported before 1991 are recapitulated by the authors in the Sage book.

The major themes presented in this important work are--that EZs are a tool and not a panacea, that there are several empirical findings showing that EZs have positive results in many cases with mixed results in other cases, and that there remains much to be learned and more significant studies to be made on the subject of EZs.

The first book by Butler covers the intellectual roots of EZs as the conception of British planning expert, Peter Hall. The second book by Sage Publications provides a chapter on the intellectual roots written by Peter Hall himself. Both Butler and Hall describe the transition from academic theory to public policy in Great Britain. Butler's works provided the intellectual foundations for establishing EZs in America coupled with the economic incentive policy initiatives of Jack Kemp. Other countries either have adopted the Hong Kong model in part or have utilized incentive based economic programs with varying and similar characteristics, but have done so out of political and economical necessity, instead of arising from published scholarly input.

MAJOR STUDIES

The major studies on EZs in the United States have been mostly case studies plus a few comparative studies of differing states and a national study. Although, the number of major studies remain relatively few, these initial studies have addressed important areas, which are (1) employment impacts, (2) benefits versus costs, (3) relocation versus creation and expansion, and (4) evaluation of EZs.

EMPLOYMENT IMPACTS

There are three major employment impact case studies that stand out in the literature. Unfortunately, all three of these studies have methodological problems, but do offer some interesting efforts at getting at some conclusions. However, the poor methodology makes the prevailing conclusions of these studies unfounded, but some of their findings, which are unaffected by their faulty final analyses, are of interest. One employment impact study is on Maryland, and the other two employment impact studies are on Illinois. It is worth noting that two of three major employment impact studies published in the literature are on Illinois, even though another study by Klemens (1991) stated a need for more and better data to generate any substantial evaluations and conclusions of the Illinois EZ program.

The study by Grasso and Crosse (1991) was a study conducted by the U.S. General Accounting Office (1988) on three EZs in Maryland. Congressmen Kemp and Garcia had requested this study of GAO, which is an arm of congress. The purpose of the study was to analyze what effects federal *income* tax incentives would have on EZs if added to existing state programs. Since 1982, Maryland has had state income tax incentives along with property tax incentives for EZs, so by reasons of close proximity to Washington, D.C., a long term program (compared to the average state program), and an income tax credit program, Maryland was chosen for this case study.

The findings of the Maryland study were that employment impacts were not statistically significant when businesses relocating to the EZs were eliminated from the data base. The reasoning was that these firms were not aware of the EZ incentives when making their location decisions. This is faulty methodology for these reasons:

1. The businesses that relocated into the EZs utilized the incentives after locating in the EZs. Since this study was to evaluate the effectiveness of incentives, and not to determine the decision-making factors in business location, these businesses were separated out of the study without good cause. Additionally, it is very common in most states for businesses to be unaware

of EZ incentives, as they are not extensively marketed by government officials.

2. Eliminating some of the valid data from relocated firms that represents a significant number of the new jobs created in the EZs, especially jobs created through the utilization of EZ incentives, is dubious at best.

3. There was statistical significance on employment impacts for all businesses utilizing the EZ incentives, so it appears there was an effort to generate negative results by using faulty criteria to separate out some of the positive results "after-the-fact." Thus, their original findings (but not final conclusions) are of great interest.

Another point worth noting is that since non-participating businesses were included in the interviews and the data base, biases against the EZ program by non-participating businesses could have influenced the researchers decision on eliminating valid data from the relocated firms that participated after their relocation.

The study by Redfield and McDonald (1991) on the employment impacts of EZs in Illinois found that not all businesses utilized the EZ incentives even when eligible. There was about a 50-50 split between those businesses that do and don't utilize the incentives. The reasons for not utilizing the incentives by those eligible businesses that did not, were shown by the following responses: (A) 51% were unaware of the incentives, (B) 24% said it was not worth the time and effort to go through the red tape, and (C) 23% felt the incentives were not relevant to them.

The study found that employment impacts were not statistically significant. Unfortunately, the methodology was weak because it incorrectly combined the results of both participating and non-participating businesses in the use of EZ incentives in the conclusion. They did this by including all investors, even those who did not utilize EZ incentives. However, their findings do show that the firms utilizing the incentives (1) had the greatest amount of investment, and (2) had created and retained most of the jobs in the EZs. Thus, EZ employment impacts appear to be of relevance by appropriately excluding those firms that did not utilize the EZ incentives.

Another study on Illinois by Esparza and Williams (1990) came up with the same basic conclusion as Redfield and McDonald (1991) of finding no statistical significance on the employment impacts of EZs. Unfortunately, this study, as the other, did not differentiate between firms utilizing EZ incentives and those not utilizing EZ incentives. Again, the firms not utilizing EZ incentives skew any data results in a negative direction when analyzing employment impacts. One noteworthy comment on this last case study on employment impacts is that it had an ideological undertone of dissuading Japanese investment in firms that are eligible for EZ incentives in Illinois.

Ironically, these three employment impact studies have methodological problems by reasons of faulty exclusion and inclusion. The Maryland study excludes the relocating firms who have utilized the EZ incentives. The two Illinois studies include all investing firms even when they have not utilized the EZ incentives. Contrary to their claims, these studies are not effectively measuring the employment impacts of EZ incentives. So this methodological inaccuracy limits their usefulness in developing effective public policies.

Also, a minor study worth noting (to add to the other three major studies) is an employment impact analysis by B.M. Rubin and Wilder (1989), which was done on Evansville, Indiana using a shift-share method. The study concluded that outside factors contributed to the job growth in the zone, more so than any factors inside the zone, since job growth occurred in the region at-large. Unfortunately, this study only analyzed a single zone while discussing EZ programs in general and failed to account for the fact that unemployment dropped nationally and regionally during the 1980s.

Lastly, the single case study on Portland, Oregon in Part Two gives additional evidence that EZ incentives create jobs for zone residents. The evidence shows that the majority of new hires of participating EZ businesses are zone residents.

BENEFITS VERSUS COSTS

The most significant study on a benefit-cost or cost-benefit analysis was authored by Marilyn Marks Rubin (1990, 1991), plus Rubin and Trawinski (1990), for New Jersey's Urban EZs as noted earlier. By including a moderate multiplier effect, the costs run about $3,000 per job created, and $1.90 is generated in public revenues as a benefit for every $1.00 of tax incentive expended. With a high multiplier effect, the benefit ratio is $5.20 to $1.00. With no multiplier effect, the benefit ratio is $.70 to $1.00 in direct public revenues. Thus, by including the total direct and indirect benefits and costs, a positive analysis is demonstrated. However, Rubin does point out that the substantial benefits of reduced welfare costs and other public and community benefits, as well as any spill over benefits and costs, are not included in the analysis.

Another noteworthy effort at conducting a benefit-cost analysis was the study authored by Logan, Jr. and Barron (1991) on EZs in Florida. Their study provides a very positive result with a low cost of $520 per job created, and Florida's income tax credit for corporations was the primary incentive utilized in the EZ program. However, this study could be argued to be a fiscal-impact statement and not a full-fledged benefit-cost analysis, since it was not a scholarly study by academicians and did not use sophisticated methodology.

Lastly, the study on Illinois by Redfield and McDonald (1991) concluded that it was extremely difficult to gather sufficient data to conduct a benefit-cost analysis along with their employment impact study, therefore the authors were unable to do so.

RELOCATION VERSUS CREATION AND EXPANSION

There is one major comparative study (Elling and Sheldon 1991) that stands out on the question--does EZ business growth occur by firms that are created and expanded from within, or by firms that relocate from the outside? As noted earlier, some of the debate on EZs is centered on the question if EZs are a tool for true economic growth or just a zero sum game of insider winners and outside losers in the location of businesses.

The important study by Elling and Sheldon (1991), as noted earlier, analyzed 47 EZs in the midwest states of Illinois, Indiana, Kentucky, and Ohio. The results show that the majority of the new business activities in EZs are (A) by expansion of existing firms at between 55-66%; (B) by creation of new firms at between 21-31%; and (C) by relocation of outside firms to the inside at between 7-16%.

A minor study worth noting was one authored by Dabney (1991) on eight zones in eight states, which came up with the conclusion that EZ incentives have little impact on the relocation decisions of firms. However, this study had a restrictive scope as it did not distinguish any incentive influences on small versus large firms, nor did it account for the amount of development activity that occurs through creation and expansion.

Also worth noting was another minor study by Gusskind (1990), which focussed primarily on Bloomington, Illinois and secondarily on Jersey City, New Jersey. It concluded that most EZ firms have been attracted from the outside and are not developed from within. This is the opposite conclusion from what the other studies found. Unfortunately, this study failed to account for the expansion of existing firms, which is the greatest indicator for new business activity, and it only considered newly created versus relocated firms. Thus, its conclusions are unreliable due to excluding the firms that actively expanded and represented much of the job growth in the zones.

Lastly, the single case study on Portland, Oregon in Part Two gives additional evidence that EZ incentives provide companies with an enhanced ability to grow from within an EZ, and are not primarily used to attract companies from other localities. The evidence shows that all participating EZ companies have vastly expanded, while none have relocated to the Portland EZ from other localities.

PROGRAM EVALUATION

There are three major contributions to the evaluation of EZs as a program. All three studies emphasize entirely different aspects of the EZ program. The landmark study by Erickson and Friedman (1990, 1991) emphasized (1) the number and kind of incentives for the zones, (2) the number of zones in each state, (3) the number of designation criteria for zones in each state, and (4) the number of new jobs created in the zones correlated with many variables.

The conclusion by the authors is that the states *concentrating* their efforts on a few zones with greater designation criteria and greater amounts of economic incentives, tend to "create more new jobs" than states mandating dozens of zones with few designation criteria and few incentives. This study was formulated into two parts--a set and a subset. The set aggregated data for 17 states and 357 zones. The subset aggregated data for 14 states and 90 zones. Most of the conclusions were found through this subset. Other conclusions worth noting are that EZs (1) are not sweatshops, (2) are not exploited by large corporations as tax havens for relocation, and (3) are not underutilized by the manufacturing industry as feared by opponents of EZs.

The major study by Brintnall and Green (1988, 1991) evaluated the degree of public and private cooperation, as well as the emphasis on public management versus private involvement. This study measured each state by giving scores and it found a mixture of results. Five states (all southern) had a hands-off approach for both public and private. Four states in four different regions had a state-managed approach. Four states in three different regions had a private involvement approach. Four states in three different regions had an activist approach, with both a strong public and a strong private emphasis. Also worth noting is the fact that one of the authors of this study, Michael Brintnall, has been contracted by the nationally renown certified public accountant (CPA) firm, Price-Waterhouse, which has contracted with HUD to develop an evaluation and data program that can be applicable to EZ programs throughout the country.

Another major evaluation study is a thorough legal review by Wolf (1989a, 1989b, 1990, 1991) on the judicial and attorneys general decisions on issues involving state EZ programs. Wolf has universally found EZs to be considered valid, to have governmental authority, and to be legally eligible for incentives mandated by state legislation even when the language has potential conflicts with state law.

RELATIONSHIP OF THE STUDY WITH THE LITERATURE

The works cited in the literature review account for many of the important references in this study. There are 92 important sources of information that are referenced throughout this study, and the references listed in the back of this book serve as possibly the best resource guide ever compiled on EZs and on other pertinent scholarship applicable to EZs. The references focus only on in-depth discussions and analyses, which help to make this study most useful in content for any researcher of EZs.

Again, this national study in Part One and the single case study in Part Two help to fill the gap in the literature on discovering the outcomes of EZs and their impacts on employment. Chapter I provides a historical and up-to-date chronological description of EZs, which is not found in any one source of the literature. Chapter II proveids the complete economic and theoretical framework of EZs, which is not found in any one source of the literature. Chapter III describes the original design and analytical techniques of deriving EZ outcomes and characteristics, which are not found in the literature. Chapter IV provides a data base on EZ characteristics and outcomes, which is not found in the literature. Chapter V provides the hypothetical and empirical tests on the outcomes of EZs, impacts on employment, and influences between EZs, which are not found in the literature. Chapter VI provides a predictive model on predicting the outcomes of EZs and, most importantly, for the policy-making of EZs, which is not found in the literature. Chapter VII (or Part Two) provides the employment outcomes of zone residents and participating businesses of a specific EZ, which are not found in the literature. In sum, the author's ground breaking work, in whole and in each part, fills much of the void and moves the literature another major step forward in the published scholarship on EZs.

CHAPTER III.

RESEARCH DESIGN

HYPOTHESES

The development of the hypotheses is based upon the search for findings and results that have never before been investigated. As noted earlier, EZs have never been sufficiently analyzed for employment impacts before this study, and the purpose of this study is to contribute something of value to the field of knowledge in public policy research. To do so, the first research question must address the results of the employment impacts of EZs. If the findings show that there are statistically significant impacts for employment with varying degrees of success between EZs, then a series of follow-up variables, based upon a theoretical development of factors or characteristics that most likely would vary the effect or employment impact, could be tested for the degree of influence (individually and collectively) on the different outcomes between EZs. Thus, the hypotheses are developed with these assumptions.

LIST OF HYPOTHESES

The economic theories, economic goals, and literature review presented in the last chapter provide the bases and theoretical underpinnings for predicting outcomes and findings with directional hypotheses in this study. Each directional hypothesis predicts a cause and effect relationship between the independent and dependent variables. As programmed for pure research methodology, the statistical analyses utilize null hypotheses, which predict no cause and effect relationships, when computing the results. These statistical results either reject or not reject the null hypotheses. These outcomes are then interpreted into the directional hypotheses, which are confirmed or disconfirmed through this method of inferential hypotheses testing. A predictive model of employment impacts is then developed by confirming many of the hypotheses, and useful knowledge is also gained by disconfirming any of the hypotheses. The following seven hypotheses, which predict causal links, are presented in priority order for analyses:

1. The difference in unemployment between Enterprise Zones and their surrounding communities has been significantly decreased by EZ activity.

2. The change in the difference in unemployment between EZs and their surrounding communities is proportional to the period of time since EZ designation.

3. The change in the difference in unemployment between EZs and their surrounding communities is proportional to the number of EZ incentives.

4. The change in the difference in unemployment between EZs and their surrounding communities is proportional to the kind of EZ incentives.

5. The change in the difference in unemployment between EZs and their surrounding communities is proportional to variations in EZ land use (i.e., percentages of residential, commercial, industrial, open space, and other).

6. The change in the difference in unemployment between EZs and their surrounding communities is proportional to EZ population density.

7. The change in the difference in unemployment between EZs and their surrounding communities is proportional to EZ geographic size.

The first hypothesis is a comparison of the unemployment rates between EZs and their surrounding communities, and is the foundation of this study. Surrounding communities constitute the control group. The result of testing the first hypothesis on Unemployment Impact (as long as the results show the statistical significance that confirms the directional hypothesis) forms the dependent variable for the testing of the differences between EZs in the remaining six hypotheses. Thus, the testing of hypotheses is an investigation of the unemployment rate differences between EZs and their surrounding communities, and of the differences between those EZs that have substantial employment impacts and those that do not.

The additional six hypotheses compare EZs with EZs, while utilizing significant independent variables as the basis for finding the causes of measurably significant differences in their employment impacts. As shown in the hypotheses, these six independent variables are Time, Number of Incentives, Kind of Incentives, Land Use, Population, and Size. No other study has tested for these important variables in a research design of measuring the employment impacts or unemployment rates of EZs.

In determining the differences of employment impacts between EZs in hypotheses 2 through 7, the first three independent variables represent *interventionist* characteristics, i.e. the length of time that incentives have been established, the quantity of incentives, and the type of incentives that are available for EZs. The last three independent variables represent *descriptive* characteristics, i.e. the development, habitation, and boundary of EZs.

One key element to comparing the differences between EZs is that locational differences are accounted for and neutralized in the analysis. This forms a more stable and precise measurement unit in testing the last six hypotheses. Locational differences are accounted for by measuring the "change in the difference," or by comparing the unemployment changes within EZs (the study group) to the changes throughout their surrounding communities (the control group), instead of merely calculating the differences in unemployment between EZs without regard for their surrounding communities.

In this way, the comparative advantages and disadvantages, which affect employment in one region but not in another, are statistically controlled. Other than the varying tax rates between areas, as noted in Chapter II, there are three additional comparative factors. These are: (1) land and natural resources, (2) physical capital and infrastructure, and (3) skilled labor and training (Schmidt 1993). Thus, the influences of varying regional economic and employment factors between paired sets of EZs and their surrounding communities are comparatively neutralized by measuring the "change in the difference."

As noted earlier, it is anticipated, due to economic theories, economic goals, and partial results gathered from studies in the literature review, that many of the directional hypotheses will be confirmed, especially the first hypothesis that addresses the employment impacts of EZs. With the economic incentives of EZs, it is premised that unemployment rates will be reduced more significantly than their surrounding communities.

It is premised that the different outcomes between EZs addressed in the second hypothesis will be the result of the length of time, since there is often a "lag time" for tax incentives to cause an effect in economic development (Benson 1986). In the third and fourth hypotheses, it is premised that the amount and type of incentives will determine the results of EZs, due to the quantity and nature of the economic incentives available to employers and/or employees.

Due to the influences of the economies of scale and business districts, it is premised that the fifth hypotheses on land development could possibly be confirmed, at least for industrial or commercial areas. Supporting this premise is the fact that Great Britain began their EZ programs in small business "industrial parks," and the Erickson, Friedman, and McCluskey (1989) report to the U.S. Department of Commerce indicated that manufacturing areas had fared very well in an evaluation of EZs.

Due to the major population and size differences between urban and rural locations, the sixth and seven hypotheses on the number of residents and the dimension for EZs are both premised to possibly cause a change in the effect. The postulate of the major differences between urban and rural areas causing a change on the impact of employment is also applied to the fifth hypothesis on land development. As noted earlier, even the disconfirming of any hypotheses that predict changes between EZ outcomes, does contribute to a greater understanding of what does not influence the employment impacts of EZs.

DATA SOURCE

This study utilizes a secondary data source collected in June 1989 by HUD. A copy of the data set was obtained by loading, transferring, and downloading computer files from a modem connection between Washington, D.C. and Portland, Oregon. It was stored in coded and structured American Standard Code for Information Interchange (ASCII) files for universal data program conversion and statistical manipulation. The ASCII files required some cleaning up of some minor miscoding of the data. This clean up procedure is a common practice when utilizing ASCII file data sets.

The data was collected by telephone interviews, which were conducted by HUD personnel with EZ administrators or managers throughout the country. The interview was a follow-up after the questionnaire had been mailed to each EZ administrator or manager. This insured that the respondents had ample opportunity to review the questions and to provide the most thorough and accurate answers to the questionnaire as possible. No respondent was asked to provide a spontaneous answer for any question. This is the "pre-contact" and "pre-letter" method, which provides for a higher quality of data collection (Frey, 1983). This strengthens the reliability of the respondents answers. HUD had quality control over the interviewers as the phone interviews and data collection took place in their headquarters in Washington, D.C..

The survey instrument provided for data on questions involving EZ characteristics, impacts, and incentives. Even though HUD expended much resources in their data collection effort, this data has never been thoroughly analyzed. This data has been made available to the author specifically for the purpose of this study. There were twenty-three (23) states selected into a cluster group for having the purest EZ legislation and for having active EZ programs among the states. All of the 336 units or EZs in the cluster group were interviewed in this survey. Obviously, those states with the largest numbers of EZs would have more respondents in the data collection by using this all-inclusive sample technique. About a half dozen of the 336 EZ programs did not respond to the survey, so these non-responses were zeroed out.

Local governmental officials generated the data by calculating unemployment rates with percentages of unemployment claims, and by using resident addresses, zip codes, and census tracts where appropriate. Although, the State of Illinois provided data by using an in-person sample survey method, which is the same door-to-door method used by the U.S. Department of Labor, Bureau of Labor Statistics, in collecting unemployment data for cities. Since calculating unemployment rates based on unemployment insurance claims (UICs) for EZs and their surrounding communities can be a very difficult process, the questionnaire was first sent by mail and then later the data was collected by phone survey, thus giving each EZ respondent ample time and opportunity to research and prepare answers for each question, including those relating to unemployment. Similarly, the research study on Maryland by Grasso and Crosse (1991) for the U.S. General Accounting Office (GAO) used UICs for their employment analysis of three EZs in Maryland.

The officials at HUD felt that collecting data from EZ administrators was preferable to collecting data from EZ participating and non-participating businesses. This strengthens the validity by going directly to the program representatives (EZ administrators), since these respondents understand the applicability of the questions and answers to their EZ programs. The GAO study can be highly criticized for gathering data from possible biased business owners, especially from the non-participating business owners who have an antagonistic feeling about the incentives for participating businesses (Wolf, 1989b).

However, in some cases EZ administrators may be biased against (not for) EZ activity, since these individuals tend to be from planning departments or finance officials. Local bureaucratic planners are schooled in previous governmental intervention and grant programs, and tend to not have free market and deregulatory instincts. Local finance officers are very reluctant to part with revenue and tend to calculate EZ costs (especially revenue losses) very highly to minimize the EZ benefits.

Since local governmental officials would more likely be biased against EZs instead of for EZs, this gives any positive impacts by EZs a stronger basis for representation, as the data would not be a result of mere wishful thinking and selective manipulation by respondents. Another strong point in the research design of this study is that the collected data is based on many years of EZ experience, so more and more results, be they pro or con, are revealed in the data. Any public policy program takes *time* for its initial implementation and then for its subsequent outcomes to be produced and measured, and this is especially true for tax and economic incentives (Benson 1986).

Additional secondary data sources are derived from the Erickson and Friedman (1991) study and the U.S. Department of Housing and Urban Development (1992) summary. Both of them were used to construct the independent variables on the Number and Kind of Incentives for each state.

Finally, the author has some strong concerns about the HUD metholodolgy of using unemployment estimates generated by distant, decentralized, and local governmental offices. It would have been better to have trained employees by HUD or contracted professionals derive the data through a systematic and centrally controlled process. In spite of the drawback, the author feels that it is important to publish the results of this national study, and to be conservative in elaborating any positive findings.

QUESTIONNAIRE

The first two pages of the telephone survey instrument gave specific instructions to the interviewers on techniques and procedures for data gathering. There was nothing unusual about these interviewer instructions. Page three was the first page of survey questions and constitutes the part of the questionnaire that was used in this study, since this page had the "meaty" questions relating to unemployment and demographics. An adaptation of these key questions can be found in Appendix B. It is worth noting that the ten additional pages of survey questions that were not utilized in this particular study could be analyzed in further research on

EZ activity.

As stated earlier, the survey instrument was provided to each EZ administrator through a pre-contact mailing with a cover letter of instructions, and later the interviewers phoned each respondent and collected the data by writing down the responses to the same questions asked over the phone. This combination made the interviews smooth and expeditious as they were carried out.

As shown in Appendix B, the first section of the questionnaire is an introductory section that requests "local zone characteristics" with the zone name, locality, and designation date. An independent variable was developed on the question regarding designation date. This question enabled the author to compose an independent variable called, Period of Time (in Months), which determined the length of time that each EZ was active.

A succeeding question on unemployment rates for the EZs and their corresponding surrounding communities at designation and currently (currently meaning June 1989 when the survey was completed), enabled the author to compose independent variables comparing the study group (EZs) to a control group (surrounding communities). Thus, the author could measure the effectiveness of EZs on employment by using a before and after "time study design," with both the study and control groups.

Additional independent variables were derived from Population, Geographic Size (in Square Miles), and Land Use questions to make comparisons between EZs. As noted earlier, and separate from the questionnaire, the research study by Erickson and Friedman (1991) and the summary by the U.S. Department of Housing and Urban Development (1992) were utilized in providing independent variables on the Number and Kind of Incentives for each state and local EZ program. The details of these incentive variables will be discussed in the next two chapters.

METHODOLOGY

Statistical analyses are to be used to measure the significance and explain the variance of the independent variables, and to predict the outcome of the dependent variable from the data set. The specific techniques will begin with a review of the distributions and frequencies of cases, and then proceed with difference of means tests (T-tests), an analysis of variance (ANOVA), a correlation matrix, simple regression and multiple regression stepwise analyses, and a residual analysis.

Each of these analytical methods has an intent. The frequencies give a preliminary indication on the results. The correlations give an indication of the links between variables. The difference of means tests measure for significance. The analysis of variance measures for a comparison of means between influential and nominal variables. The regression analysis measures for significance, explains the variance, measures and orders and compares the coefficients or the influence of independent variables on the dependent variable, and is used to build a predictive model for the weighted values of each significant variable. The successful completion of this predictive model constitutes an invaluable contribution of this study to public policy research. The residual analysis compares the actual and predicted outcomes for each EZ case in applying the predictive model specifically within the data set. Lastly, the predictive model is translated and applied in general to all EZs outside of the data set.

To test for the first hypothesis on the Unemployment Impact between EZs and their surrounding communities, a paired difference of means test with ratio data is used to test for statistical significance. The paired or matched T-test is appropriate for this analysis, which allows for testing a subset of the data set.

The Maryland study on EZ employment by Grasso and Crosse (1991), which was reported to the U.S. General Accounting Office (1988), tested for statistical significance by using an interrupted time series (ITS) analysis for testing a "moving difference of means." Thus, difference of means testing has been used for EZ employment questions. Since the author's study utilizes a before and after time study on EZs with a control group (surrounding communities), a difference of means test is appropriate for this data set.

This first test on the difference in the change of unemployment between EZs and their surrounding communities is fundamental to testing the remaining hypotheses, since the research model requires that the dependent variable be statistically significant. Additionally, to test for the third and fourth hypotheses on the Number and Kind of Incentives, independent difference of means tests (independent T-tests) are also used for both hypotheses, while an analysis of variance (ANOVA) is used for the fourth hypothesis to compare the specific incentives that have the greatest impacts. These influential variables are parsimoniously selected for this ANOVA technique.

To test for all of the remaining hypotheses (2-7) by measuring the simultaneous influence of all significant variables, multiple regression analysis is utilized to derive this vital information. Interval data is used in hypotheses 2, 3, 6, and 7, which is appropriate for regression analysis. Ratio data is used in hypothesis 5 and is equally appropriate. Nominal data is used in hypotheses 3 and 4, and it is converted into dummy variables (dichotomous categories or groups) as needed to be appropriate for the analytical techniques.

The study by Erickson and Friedman (1989, 1991) at Pennsylvania State University using 1985-86 national HUD data, utilized multiple regression stepwise techniques to measure correlation coefficients and to explain the variances of the variables. Erickson and Friedman (1991) evaluated overall characteristics of EZs to better explain state programs and activities occurring within the targeted areas. Regression analysis was also utilized in the Four State Perspective study by Elling and Sheldon (1991). Elling and Sheldon (1991) researched the jobs created and retained by EZ firms, along with EZ investment dollars, by categories of "all firms, new firms, expanding firms, and relocating firms." Thus, multiple regression stepwise techniques are appropriate in analyzing the many variables proposed in this study.

The three previous scholarly studies cited above are the most comparable to the author's research methods. However, the author's study went beyond these other studies by building a predictive model for universal application in the United States, and by utilizing residual analysis, which is an analytical, case by case, follow-up to the regression analysis. Thus, each EZ in this study will be compared to the predictive model. Again, the most valuable contribution of this methodology was the statistical development of a predictive model on the performance of EZs for those variables proved significant. This analytical model is applicable to predicting and evaluating outcomes on all EZs, including those designated in the past, present, and future.

Lastly, the level of significance selected in the methodology for this study is at the commonly accepted probability of 5% or .05 and below. The level of significance refers to the probability of rejecting a null hypothesis when in fact it is true. As noted earlier, this significance level or statistical result for each test is interpreted by inference into confirming or disconfirming each directional hypothesis. Thus, a probability value of .05 or below will reject the null hypothesis and confirm the directional hypothesis, while a probability value greater than the significance level standard will neither reject the null hypothesis nor confirm the directional hypothesis.

CHAPTER IV.

DATA REVIEW

CASE SELECTION

LIST OF CRITERIA

The criteria for the case selection was based on the five following parameters, with four parameters relating to employment factors and one parameter relating to a non-employment factor:

1. All appropriate questions had to answered by the respondent, especially the questions involving unemployment at the date of designation and currently (date of survey) for both the zone and the surrounding community (see Appendix B). All partial responses were deemed inappropriate, since different sets and subsets of cases would be answering different questions.

2. There had to be at least a 5% unemployment rate in the zone at designation, since this is the "natural rate of unemployment," which has historically and narrowly oscillated at 5% during most of this century with labor-market transitions (Vedder and Galloway 1993). By definition, it does not make sense to create an EZ in an area with less than a natural rate of unemployment.

3. The unemployment rate in the EZ had to be higher than in the surrounding community. By definition, it does not make sense for government to create

a targeted area for economic growth that has greater employment than the rest of the community.

4. The change in the difference in unemployment (between an EZ and its surrounding community) had to be less than double digits or 10%, as data above this amount was seen as showing a couple of outliers with enormous differences from the great body of the data with an average of 1.5%. It did not make sense to automatically attribute these outliers of up to 20%, which were enormously positive indicators in the data, to the impact of EZs. By eliminating the outliers, the results were prevented from being skewed in favor of EZs. As noted in Chapter I and II, the debate on the merits of EZs is very heated, so the author did not want to base any positive impacts on a couple of cases skewing the results.

5. The dimension of an EZ had to be less than 50 square miles. This allowed for both urban and rural areas. By definition, an EZ is a narrowly targeted area, both urban and rural. So, any area larger than 50 square miles was not considered a targeted program. There were no cases between 50-100 square miles that met the four employment parameters. Thus a few cases with hundreds and thousands of square miles were eliminated as falling outside of the EZ definition. These few cases were regional sections of the states and were outliers to the data base.

The parameters narrowed the number of cases (or EZs) to 60. The first parameter narrowed down most of the cases, and the other four parameters narrowed them further. This gave the author the best possible set of cases to measure the outcome with validity and reliability. It appears that the local government officials responding to the total survey could not easily answer all of the questions on unemployment involving changes and differences. This is not surprising, since not all of the state legislatures mandate a report on unemployment in EZs and surrounding communities each year.

Another issue with the unemployment data is it appears that some of the EZ administrators may have used 1980 census tract data to answer all of the unemployment questions, which would show no change in unemployment. This could skew the results against EZs. Yet, these eleven cases were left in the data set, since, first of all, there is no definite proof one way or the other that the EZ administrators used only 1980 census data, and secondly, any positive impact of EZs could not be falsely attributed by critics to case filtering and manipulation. Thus, any impact of EZs on unemployment must be major to show a positive result. Also, any positive result would not be subject to overstatement in the findings of this study.

A strong recommendation resulting from this survey and data review is that the federal government should mandate an annual report by each EZ jurisdiction on the outcomes, especially the outcome of unemployment changes and differences between EZs and their surrounding communities. This would be most appropriate for federal EZs receiving economic incentives, although the current federal legislation (with only modest incentives to influence their impacts) would result in only nine case studies.

DATA OBSERVATIONS

Table I on page 72 lists the states (14) and the number of EZs in each state represented in the study. The State of Illinois had a total of 16 EZs (or 27% of all cases), which was over twice as many EZs as any other state. The Midwest was the region with the largest number of EZs at 30 (or 50% of all cases), which came from four states. The South was the region with the most states at five, which accounted for 18 EZs (or 30% of all cases). The East had two states and eight EZs (or 13.3% of all cases). The West had three states and four EZs (or 6.7% of all cases).

It appears from the data in Table 1 that the State of Illinois and the Midwest region, along with the South region, have substantial representation on the results of this study. The East and West regions have moderate, but important, representation. The regional breakdowns in the study sample are similar to the actual EZ activities legislated in the states throughout the country, with the Midwest and South having many EZ programs and the West having few EZ programs. The exceptions are that Illinois is overrepresented in the Midwest and the East is slightly underrepresented as a region when comparing the data with actual legislated EZ programs. But overall, it is a solid study sample.

Finally, Table I shows that the total number of responses (60) based on the criteria for case selection is at a 18% response rate. Another interesting observation is that 23 states participated in the survey, but only 14 states provided complete responses based on the criteria for a 61% response rate. Again, the method of pre-contact by mail and follow-up interview by phone enabled nearly a fifth of all respondents to obtain the requested unemployment data for the survey. As noted earlier, some EZ programs are better able to produce the requested data than others, due to reporting mandates for the state legislatures. Illinois EZs reported unemployment rates through an annual survey, which is why it had greater representation as shown in Table I.

As noted in the selection criteria, Table II on pages 73-75 shows the unemployment rates where the zone is higher than the surrounding community at designation and the zone has at least a 5% unemployment rate at designation. It is organized state by state with unemployment rates for the zone at designation (ZNUMPDES), the surrounding community at designation (CUMPDES), the zone currently (ZNUMPCUR), the surrounding community currently (CUMPCUR), the difference in the zone between designation and currently (dz), and the difference in the surrounding community between designation and currently (dc). The variables dz and dc have been created by utilizing the four previous variables in the HUD survey.

The means show that the zones have double digit unemployment rates both at designation and currently, while the surrounding communities have less than double digit rates. The mean difference in the zones (dz) has a huge decrease of 3.8%, while the mean difference in the surrounding communities (dc) has a decrease of 2.3%. This illustrates that unemployment decreased for all areas (which is correlated to the fact that overall unemployment dropped in the 1980s), but it decreased much more dramatically and sharply in EZs.

Table III on pages 76-78 shows the difference of unemployment rates between changes within the zones and changes within their surrounding communities, which is variable dz-dc. By utilizing the variables dz and dc in Table II, the variable dz-dc (ordz minus dc) has been created by taking the difference in the zone between designation and currently, and *subtracting* the difference in the surrounding community between designation and currently. The mean result of dz-dc (or the change in the difference of means) is 1.5%. In other words, the average impact of EZs on unemployment, when taking into account the locational differences of surrounding communities, is a decrease in the unemployment rate of 1.5% greater than what occurred in the surrounding communities. Thus, the impact of the EZs on decreasing unemployment is 65% greater than the decline in the surrounding communities.

The variables dz and dc, as shown in Tables II and III, formulated a paired T-test in the next chapter, which was is to measure the statistical significance of the first hypothesis on the impact of EZs on unemployment. As noted in Chapter III, the result of this test, then became the dependent variable to test the remaining hypotheses on the differences between EZs.

Continuing on Table III, it shows that the average length of time since designation for each zone is 38 months, or three years and two months. The time period of EZs is somewhat of a limiting factor, since programs only began in the 1980s and the survey was conducted in June of 1989, yet there is a varied enough difference in time periods to measure for the significant influence on EZs. A good dispersement of the cases is illustrated through the following breakdown of the number of zones grouped by the time period in years: 0-1 years = 12 zones; 1-2 years = 6 zones; 2-3 years = 10 zones; 3-4 years = 9 zones; 4-5 years = 9 zones; and 5-6 years = 14 zones.

Again the incentive variables have been created by utilizing the study by Erickson and Friedman (1991) and the summary by the U.S. Department of Housing and Urban Development (1992), and added to the data base. The average quantity of incentives is 4.9, or just under 5 incentives per zone. The subcategories of the Number of Incentives show that 60% of the zones have a high Rank (5-8 incentives is high and 1-4 incentives is low), 73% have employer Income Tax incentives, and 78% have employer Property Tax incentives.

There are 12 types of incentives that have been utilized by EZ programs throughout the country (Erickson and Friedman 1991). In Table III, the highest Number of Incentives for a state (8 for Missouri) is only two-thirds of the possible incentives, while the average number of incentives is only four-tenths. However, it should be noted that the apportioned and qualitative strength of each type of incentive between the states, such as varying percentages and amounts of tax abatements and credits, is not represented in Table III.

All of these variables (dz - dc or Unemployment Impact, the Period of Time or Months, the Number and Rank of Incentives, and the Kind of Incentives or Property and Income Taxes) in Table III will be thoroughly discussed in Chapter V. All of these variables proved to be statistically significant (individually or in combination) and therefore were implemented in the analyses and predictive models in Chapters V and VI.

Table IV on pages 79-81 shows developed and undeveloped land percentages by the zones. Only one zone (Springfield, Ohio) did not complete land use data. On average, the vast majority of Land Use in the zones are Residential, Commercial, and Industrial areas with mean totals of 28.8%, 21.1%, and 26.5% respectively. This proportional land development was expected as EZs are most often targeted for these specific areas of mixed land development in communities, especially those with combined neighborhoods and business districts.

The categories of Open and Other property uses are not specifically defined in the survey, so some misunderstanding by the respondents may have resulted with agricultural land, which could be arbitrarily put into either category. This is indicated in the cases where "Other" property use had mainly zero percentages reported with a few cases showing very high percentages. For the most part, this did not affect the results as Residential, Commercial, and Industrial are self-explanatory. Additionally, urban zones have public, vacant, and undeveloped property uses, but not agricultural; whereas, rural zones solely have the agricultural areas. So, the Open and Other property uses could be separated or lumped together accordingly (although neither grouping changed the results in the next chapter).

Table V on pages 82-84 shows two of the descriptive elements of the zones, which are Population Density and Geographic Size (in Square Miles). The average population at designation is 12,177 with an increase to 13,295 at the date of the survey. Many of the EZ administrators or managers appeared to use 1980 census data for both designation and current questions, so the populations appear unchanged. This would also nullify any shifts in population that occurred during this time frame. Thus, the population data from this survey is useful only to measure the impact of density on unemployment, and not for calculating population shifts in the equation. The calculation of the population shifts by comparing the years 1980 and 1990 is available from the U.S. Census Bureau, but this was not pertinent, available, or utilized in this study.

Several zones (Belvider, Blue Island, and Olney Illinois; McKeesport, Pennsylvania; Mount Pleasant, Texas; and Chesapeake, Virginia) do not have complete population data, but do have complete data for the unemployment questions so they are kept in the study. The largest zone in both categories of Population and Geographic Size is Columbus, County in Ohio. Columbus is many times greater in population than the other EZs and only St. Joseph, Missouri is close to it in square miles, as both zones were many times greater in size than the other EZs. However, Columbus has been maintained in the study, since it falls within the strict definition of an EZ, plus it has unemployment data on all pertinent questions in the survey. The average size of the zones was 6.5 square miles, and by removing Columbus and St. Joseph from the data set for purposes of illustration only, the average dropped mildly to 5.3 square miles. Again, this shows the targeted nature of an EZ program.

The variables derived from both Tables IV and V proved not to be statistically significant as will be discussed in the next chapter. However, these variables are interesting to review in gaining a greater understanding of EZs.

TABLE I

STATES AND NUMBER OF ZONES IN DATA SET

14 States	*Zones*
Alabama	*1*
California	*2*
Florida	*1*
Illinois	*16*
Indiana	*6*
Kentucky	*3*
Missouri	*3*
Nevada	*1*
New Jersey	*3*
Ohio	*5*
Oregon	*1*
Pennsylvania	*5*
Texas	*7*
Virginia	*6*
	60 total

Regional Distribution:

Midwest		*South*		*East*		*West*	
IL	16	TX	7	PA	5	CA	2
IN	6	VA	6	NJ	3	NV	1
OH	5	KY	3		8	OR	1
MO	3	AL	1				4
	30	FL	1				
			18				

TABLE II

UNEMPLOYMENT RATES

	ZNUMPDES	CUMPDES	ZNUMPCUR	CUMPCUR	dz	dc
ALABAMA:						
Dallas Co.	20.0	15.5	20.0	11.3	0.0	4.2
CALIFORNIA:						
Fresno	13.3	7.9	18.9	9.6	-5.6	-1.7
Pittsburgh	13.3	6.1	13.3	6.1	0.0	0.0
FLORIDA:						
Franklin	15.0	4.0	15.0	4.0	0.0	0.0
ILLINOIS:						
Belleville	6.2	5.9	11.5	11.5	-5.3	-5.6
Belvider	12.2	10.5	7.2	6.1	5.0	4.4
Blue Island	8.5	8.0	7.5	7.0	1.0	1.0
Bureau	14.1	9.9	12.8	9.0	1.3	0.9
Centralia	13.2	8.7	13.2	8.7	0.0	0.0
Danville	28.8	17.3	19.2	12.4	9.6	4.9
Dixon	11.6	9.9	9.8	7.4	1.8	2.5
East Chicago	20.2	12.9	20.2	12.9	0.0	0.0
Illiopolis	13.0	12.0	11.0	10.0	2.0	2.0
Mound City	21.0	10.0	26.0	15.0	-5.0	-5.0
Olney	22.9	8.7	14.0	9.4	8.9	-0.7
Riverbend	11.9	10.4	9.2	7.1	2.7	3.3
Rock Island	21.6	11.0	12.0	7.6	9.6	3.4
SW Madison	17.4	10.7	13.2	7.1	4.2	3.6
Urbana	12.9	6.2	10.1	4.8	2.8	1.4
Will Co.	22.6	14.0	7.0	6.2	15.6	7.8
INDIANA:						
Anderson	20.9	9.6	8.0	6.0	12.9	3.6
Elkhart	12.6	8.0	8.0	5.0	4.6	3.0
Evansville	19.0	8.7	9.0	5.4	10.0	3.3
Hammond	18.4	13.0	10.3	5.9	8.1	7.1
Madison	20.7	16.0	7.2	6.5	13.5	9.5
Michigan	18.0	12.0	8.0	5.5	10.0	6.5
KENTUCKY:						
Ashland	18.8	14.5	14.3	11.7	4.5	2.8
Campbell	12.5	7.0	9.9	5.0	2.6	2.0
Covington	13.7	10.0	10.3	8.0	3.4	2.0

TABLE II continued

UNEMPLOYMENT RATES

	ZNUMPDES	*CUMPDES*	*ZNUMPCUR*	*CUMPCUR*	*dz*	*dc*
MISSOURI:						
Brookfield	*20.7*	*13.6*	*11.3*	*9.6*	*9.4*	*4.0*
Chillicothe	*12.9*	*8.1*	*12.9*	*5.3*	*0.0*	*2.8*
St. Joseph	*20.4*	*7.0*	*16.0*	*6.5*	*4.4*	*0.5*
NEVADA:						
Las Vegas	*13.7*	*5.1*	*13.7*	*5.1*	*0.0*	*0.0*
NEW JERSEY:						
Camden	*12.5*	*7.0*	*9.9*	*5.0*	*2.6*	*2.0*
Millville	*13.0*	*11.0*	*11.8*	*9.2*	*1.2*	*1.8*
Orange City	*20.9*	*16.4*	*19.4*	*12.6*	*1.5*	*3.8*
OHIO:						
Ashland	*12.1*	*9.1*	*6.5*	*5.5*	*5.6*	*3.6*
Columbus	*13.7*	*6.3*	*8.9*	*4.8*	*4.8*	*1.5*
Fairfield	*26.6*	*14.4*	*8.5*	*5.9*	*18.1*	*8.5*
Marion Co.	*19.7*	*14.1*	*10.5*	*7.6*	*9.2*	*6.5*
Springfield	*13.3*	*5.5*	*10.0*	*5.5*	*3.3*	*0.0*
OREGON:						
Seaside	*5.9*	*5.2*	*5.9*	*5.2*	*0.0*	*0.0*
PENN-SYLVANIA:						
Johnstown	*25.5*	*24.0*	*12.0*	*8.0*	*13.0*	*16.0*
McKeesport	*19.0*	*7.0*	*18.1*	*6.0*	*0.9*	*1.0*
Monessen	*27.0*	*14.0*	*29.0*	*13.0*	*-2.0*	*1.0*
Lancaster	*22.9*	*9.9*	*12.2*	*5.5*	*10.7*	*4.4*
Reading	*7.1*	*4.0*	*6.3*	*4.2*	*0.8*	*-0.2*
TEXAS:						
Athens	*14.2*	*8.8*	*14.2*	*8.8*	*0.0*	*0.0*
Brownsville	*18.3*	*14.1*	*15.8*	*12.6*	*2.5*	*1.5*
Dimmett	*9.5*	*5.1*	*9.5*	*5.1*	*0.0*	*0.0*
Gainsville	*14.8*	*8.9*	*14.8*	*8.9*	*0.0*	*0.0*
Mount Pleasant	*8.3*	*8.0*	*8.3*	*8.2*	*0.0*	*-0.2*
San Benito	*13.0*	*11.0*	*13.0*	*11.0*	*0.0*	*0.0*
Texas City	*21.9*	*13.4*	*11.4*	*9.1*	*10.5*	*4.3*

TABLE II continued

UNEMPLOYMENT RATES

	ZNUMPDES	*CUMPDES*	*ZNUMPCUR*	*CUMPCUR*	*dz*	*dc*
VIRGINIA:						
Chesapeake	*12.0*	*6.0*	*10.0*	*4.5*	*2.0*	*1.5*
Danville	*15.0*	*8.0*	*15.0*	*8.0*	*0.0*	*0.0*
Newport	*10.1*	*5.6*	*8.6*	*4.8*	*1.5*	*0.8*
Norfolk	*14.8*	*7.7*	*10.4*	*4.2*	*4.4*	*3.5*
Saltville	14.0	12.0	10.0	8.0	4.0	4.0
Waynesboro	6.6	3.2	8.0	4.9	-1.4	-1.7
MEAN	15.9	9.9	12.1	7.6	3.8	2.3

<u>Key to Table II</u>

ZNUMPDES	=	Zone Unemployment Rate at Designation
CUMPDES	=	Surrounding Community Unemployment Rate at Designation
ZNUMPCUR	=	Zone Unemployment Rate Currently
CUMPCUR	=	Surrounding Community Unemployment Rate Currently
dz	=	Difference between ZNUMPDES and ZNUMPCUR (or the Zone Unemployment Rate at Designation minus the Zone Unemployment Rate Currently)
dc	=	Difference between CUMPDES and CUMPCUR (or the Surrounding Community Unemployment Rate at Designation minus the Surrounding Community Unemployment Rate Currently)

TABLE III

SIGNIFICANT VARIABLES

	dz-dc	*Months*	*INCENTIVES*	*Rank*	*Income*	*Property*
ALABAMA:			4	*Low*	*No*	*No*
Dallas Co.	*-4.2*	24				
CALIFORNIA:						
Fresno	*-3.9*	32	6 (N)	*High*	*Yes*	*No*
Pittsburgh	*0.0*	17	5 (W)	*High*	*Yes*	*No*
FLORIDA:			6	*High*	*No*	*Yes*
Franklin	*0.0*	29				
ILLINOIS:			6	*High*	*Yes*	*Yes*
Belleville	*0.3*	47				
Belvider	*0.6*	47				
Blue Island	*0.0*	47				
Bureau	*0.4*	23				
Centralia	*0.0*	23				
Danville	*4.7*	59				
Dixon	*-0.7*	23				
East Chicago	*0.0*	5				
Illiopolis	*0.0*	35				
Mound City	*0.0*	60				
Olney	*9.6*	23				
SW Madison	*0.6*	47				
Riverbend	*-0.6*	36				
Rock Island	*6.2*	47				
Urbana	*1.4*	47				
Will Co.	*7.8*	71				
INDIANA:			6	*High*	*Yes*	*Yes*
Anderson	*9.3*	65				
Elkhart	*1.6*	53				
Evansville	*6.7*	65				
Hammond	*1.0*	50				
Madison	*4.0*	53				
Michigan	*3.5*	65				
KENTUCKY:			3	*Low*	*Yes*	*Yes*
Ashland	*1.7*	64				
Campbell	*0.6*	31				
Covington	*1.4*	64				

TABLE III continued

SIGNIFICANT VARIABLES

	d_z-d_c	Months	INCENTIVES	Rank	Income	Property
MISSOURI:			8	High	Yes	Yes
St. Joseph	3.9	49				
Brookfield	5.4	64				
Chillicothe	-2.8	56				
NEVADA:			1	Low	No	No
Las Vegas	0.0	5				
NEW JERSEY:			6	High	Yes	No
Camden	0.6	31				
Millville	-0.6	39				
Orange City	-2.3	29				
OHIO:			5	High	Yes	Yes
Ashland	2.0	31				
Columbus	3.3	48				
Fairfield	9.6	52				
Marion Co.	2.7	7				
Springfield	3.3	26				
OREGON:			1	Low	No	Yes
Seaside	0.0	6				
PENN-SYLVANIA:			3	Low	No	Yes
Johnstown	-3.0	69				
Monessen	-3.0	8				
Lancaster	6.3	69				
McKeesport	-0.1	57				
Reading	1.0	29				
TEXAS:			4	Low	No	Yes
Athens	0.0	9				
Brownsville	1.0	9				
Dimmett	0.0	3				
Gainsville	0.0	7				
Mount Pleasant	0.2	4				
San Benito	0.0	1				
Texas City	6.2	7				

TABLE III continued

SIGNIFICANT VARIABLES

	dz-dc	Months	INCENTIVES	Rank	Income	Property
VIRGINIA:			3	Low	Yes	No
Norfolk	0.9	65				
Waynesboro	0.3	17				
Saltville	0.0	65				
Chesapeake	0.5	49				
Danville	0.0	65				
Newport	0.7	65				
MEAN	1.5	38	4.9			

Incentives Breakdown

Rank:
High   = 36 zones or 60%
Low   = 24 zones or 40%

Income:
Yes   = 44 zones or 73%
No   = 16 zones or 27%

Property:
Yes   = 47 zones or 78%
No   = 13 zones or 22%

Key to Table III

dz-dc	=	*Unemployment Impact, or the change in the Difference between the Zone and the Surrounding Community, or the Difference between the Zone Unemployment Rate at Designation and the Zone Unemployment Rate Currently "minus" the Difference between the Surrounding Community Unemployment Rate at Designation and the Surrounding Community Unemployment Rate Currently, or (ZNUMPDES - ZNUMPCUR) - (CUMPDES - CUMPCUR)*
Months	=	*Period of Time (from date of designation to currently or June 1989 survey)*
Incentives	=	*"Number" of Incentives (available through State legislation)*
Rank	=	*Group "Rank" for Number of Incentives, (1 to 4 = Low; 5 to 8 = High)*
Income	=	*Employer "Income" Tax Incentive*
Property	=	*Employer "Property" Tax Incentive*
(N)	=	*Nolan Legislation in California*
(W)	=	*Waters Legislation in California*

TABLE IV

LAND USE PERCENTAGES

	RES	COM	IND	OPEN	OTHER
ALABAMA:					
Dallas Co.	20.0	10.0	30.0	40.0	0.0
CALIFORNIA:					
Fresno	38.0	15.0	45.0	1.0	1.0
Pittsburgh	25.0	25.0	20.0	30.0	0.0
FLORIDA:					
Franklin	70.0	10.0	10.0	10.0	0.0
ILLINOIS:					
Belleville	45.0	40.0	10.0	5.0	0.0
Belvider	0.0	30.0	70.0	0.0	0.0
Blue Island	50.0	15.0	25.0	10.0	0.0
Bureau	10.0	15.0	5.0	70.0	0.0
Centralia	21.0	4.0	6.0	33.0	36.0
Danville	16.0	30.0	40.0	14.0	0.0
Dixon	36.0	4.0	22.0	35.0	3.0
East Chicago	5.0	2.2	52.7	40.1	0.0
Illiopolis	10.0	8.0	10.0	72.0	0.0
Mound City	20.0	5.0	25.0	50.0	0.0
Olney	11.0	96.8	7.2	0.0	0.0
Riverbend	10.0	5.0	51.0	34.0	0.0
Rock Island	2.0	18.0	70.0	10.0	0.0
SW Madison	22.0	3.0	39.0	36.0	0.0
Urbana	28.0	31.0	17.0	24.0	0.0
Will Co.	60.0	10.0	20.0	10.0	0.0
INDIANA:					
Anderson	67.3	3.6	7.1	6.0	16.0
Elkhart	46.0	18.0	33.0	3.0	0.0
Evansville	32.0	9.0	57.0	2.0	0.0
Hammond	23.0	3.2	56.0	15.0	2.8
Madison	32.0	24.0	28.0	16.0	0.0
Michigan	34.0	7.0	21.0	19.0	19.0
KENTUCKY:					
Ashland	25.0	40.0	30.0	5.0	0.0
Campbell	25.0	65.0	10.0	0.0	0.0
Covington	40.0	40.0	20.0	0.0	0.0

TABLE IV continued

LAND USE PERCENTAGES

	RES	COM	IND	OPEN	OTHER
MISSOURI:					
Brookfield	47.0	25.0	20.0	6.0	2.0
Chillicothe	25.0	5.0	50.0	2.0	18.0
St. Joseph	15.0	20.0	20.0	10.0	35.0
NEVADA:					
Las Vegas	55.0	10.0	5.0	30.0	0.0
NEW JERSEY:					
Camden	25.0	65.0	10.0	0.0	0.0
Millville	0.0	60.0	40.0	0.0	0.0
Orange City	50.0	23.0	17.0	10.0	0.0
OHIO:					
Ashland	20.0	25.0	35.0	18.0	2.0
Columbus	21.0	4.8	2.2	1.9	70.1
Fairfield	20.0	15.0	30.0	25.0	10.0
Marion Co.	65.0	10.0	15.0	5.0	5.0
Springfield	n/a	n/a	n/a	n/a	n/a
OREGON:					
Seaside	25.0	15.0	10.0	40.0	10.0
PENN-SYLVANIA:					
Johnstown	25.0	35.0	30.0	0.0	10.0
Lancaster	62.0	23.0	15.0	0.0	0.0
McKeesport	0.0	30.0	60.0	5.0	5.0
Monessen	10.0	20.0	60.0	10.0	0.0
Reading	29.2	16.4	54.4	0.0	0.0
TEXAS:					
Athens	45.0	30.0	10.0	15.0	10.0
Brownsville	25.0	45.0	20.0	10.0	0.0
Dimmett	2.0	1.0	2.0	2.0	93.0
Gainsville	50.0	10.0	15.0	25.0	0.0
Mount Pleasant	15.0	10.0	5.0	55.0	15.0
San Benito	35.0	15.0	25.0	25.0	0.0
Texas City	20.0	10.0	40.0	30.0	0.0

TABLE IV continued

LAND USE PERCENTAGES

	RES	*COM*	*IND*	*OPEN*	*OTHER*
VIRGINIA:					
Chesapeake	*44.0*	*14.0*	*4.0*	*20.0*	*18.0*
Danville	*30.0*	*15.0*	*25.0*	*20.0*	*0.0*
Newport	*48.0*	*8.0*	*27.0*	*1.0*	*16.0*
Norfolk	*41.0*	*35.0*	*23.0*	*1.0*	*0.0*
Saltville	*10.0*	*40.0*	*20.0*	*30.0*	*0.0*
Waynesboro	*18.0*	*25.0*	*35.0*	*12.0*	*10.0*
MEAN*	*28.8*	*21.1*	*26.5*	*17.1*	*6.9*

* Combined means slightly higher than 100% due to rounding off

Key to Table IV

RES	=	*Percentage of "Residential" Land Use*
COM	=	*Percentage of "Commercial" Land Use*
IND	=	*Percentage of "Industrial" Land Use*
OPEN	=	*Percentage of "Open" Land Use*
OTHER	=	*Percentage of "Other" Land Use*
n/a	=	*Not available*

TABLE V

POPULATION AND GEOGRAPHIC SIZE

	ZNPOPDES	ZNPOPCUR	Size
ALABAMA:			
Dallas Co.	2,000	2,000	3.7
CALIFORNIA:			
Fresno	27,000	27,000	10.0
Pittsburgh	9,161	9,161	1.6
FLORIDA:			
Franklin	4,000	4,000	1.0
ILLINOIS:			
Belleville	36,315	37,415	8.2
Belvider	3,570	n/a	6.7
Blue Island	30,000	n/a	8.0
Bureau	3,665	3,290	10.1
Centralia	17,040	7,040	6.7
Danville	6,548	6,200	4.7
Dixon	8,225	8,225	6.5
East Chicago	5,837	5,837	2.8
Illiopolis	5,500	5,500	10.0
Mound City	1,102	1,102	2.0
Olney	n/a	n/a	4.4
Riverbend	10,460	10,528	11.5
Rock Island	6,225	6,000	2.5
SW Madison	18,917	19,041	10.0
Urbana	6,125	6,125	1.8
Will Co.	54,000	54,000	10.3
INDIANA:			
Anderson	7,657	8,200	1.8
Elkhart	6,977	7,000	1.5
Evansville	7,919	7,300	2.5
Hammond	7,075	7,737	2.5
Madison	5,204	5,482	2.0
Michigan	8,000	8,000	2.9
KENTUCKY:			
Ashland	2,938	7,977	4.2
Campbell	28,505	29,240	9.5
Covington	8,082	30,630	13.4

TABLE V continued

POPULATION AND GEOGRAPHIC SIZE

	ZNPOPDES	ZNPOPCUR	Size
MISSOURI:			
Brookfield	2,961	2,961	3.5
Chillicothe	2,826	2,420	3.0
St. Joseph	29,956	32,000	41.4
NEVADA:			
Las Vegas	10,803	10,803	2.0
NEW JERSEY:			
Camden	28,505	29,240	9.4
Millville	7,581	7,951	14.0
Orange City	12,724	12,127	0.7
OHIO:			
Ashland	6,204	6,204	3.1
Columbus	223,500	211,297	44.0
Fairfield	4,483	4,300	2.0
Marion Co.	30,250	30,250	6.0
Springfield	47,078	48,600	2.3
OREGON:			
Seaside	5,735	5,735	4.1
PENN-SYLVANIA:			
Johnstown	24,000	22,000	3.5
Lancaster	13,615	14,500	2.0
McKeesport	3,659	n/a	1.1
Monessen	560	600	3.6
Reading	10,538	32,772	2.0
TEXAS:			
Athens	2,120	2,300	4.6
Brownsville	6,585	6,585	9.8
Dimmett	2,505	2,505	14.5
Gainsville	5,252	5,252	12.8
Mount Pleasant	n/a	n/a	14.4
San Benito	9,267	9,267	2.6
Texas City	6,887	6,887	9.9

TABLE V continued

POPULATION AND GEOGRAPHIC SIZE

	ZNPOPDES	ZNPOPCUR	Size
VIRGINIA:			
Chesapeake	10,388	n/a	1.6
Danville	2,139	2,139	1.0
Newport	20,586	20,960	2.6
Norfolk	25,442	25,400	3.2
Saltville	1,000	1,050	0.4
Waynesboro	2,832	2,832	0.9
MEAN	12,177	13,295	6.5

Key to Table V

ZNPOPDES	=	Population in the Zone at Designation
ZNPOPCUR	=	Population in the Zone Currently
Size	=	Geographic Square Miles of Zone
n/a	=	Not available

CHAPTER V

RESULTS OF TESTING THE HYPOTHESES

UNEMPLOYMENT IMPACT

Hypothesis 1: The difference in unemployment between Enterprise Zones and their surrounding areas has been significantly decreased by EZ activity.

PAIRED T-TEST

As discussed in chapter three, the first hypothesis on Unemployment Impact is tested by utilizing a matched or paired T-Test to analyze the means between EZs and their surrounding communities. This test measures the significance for the change in the difference of the means. To set up the variables, the difference in unemployment in the zone between designation and currently (ZNUMPDES - ZNUMPCUR = dz), is compared to the difference in unemployment in the surrounding community between designation and currently (CUMPDES - CUMPCUR = dc). The zone and its surrounding community are matched or paired in this analysis. This comparison constitutes the "change" in the difference in unemployment between the zone and its surrounding community (or dz - dc). This analysis not only tests the first hypothesis, but the result or change becomes the dependent variable for testing the remaining six hypotheses, which compare the differences between the zones.

The results for the means of the unemployment rate variables are shown in Table VI on page 86. The outcome is that the change in the difference between the

TABLE VI

PAIRED T-TEST

UNEMPLOYMENT RATES:

VARIABLES	MEAN	STANDARD DEVIATION	MINIMUM	MAXIMUM
ZNUMPDES	15.9	5.4	5.9	28.8
ZNUMPCUR	12.1	4.6	5.9	29.0
dz	3.8	5.1	-5.6	18.1
CUMPDES	9.9	3.9	3.2	24.0
CUMPCUR	7.6	2.7	4.0	15.0
dc	2.3	3.3	-5.6	16.0
dz - dc (change in differences)	1.5	3.1		

or

3.8 - 2.3 = 1.5

p = .0006

N = 60

Key to Table VI

ZNUMPDES	=	Zone Unemployment Rate at Designation
CUMPDES	=	Surrounding Community Unemployment Rate at Designation
ZNUMPCUR	=	Zone Unemployment Rate Currently
CUMPCUR	=	Surrounding Community Unemployment Rate Currently
dz	=	Difference between ZNUMPDES and ZNUMPCUR (or the Zone Unemployment Rate at Designation minus the Zone Unemployment Rate Currently)
dc	=	Difference between CUMPDES and CUMPCUR (or the Surrounding Community Unemployment Rate at Designation minus the Surrounding Community Unemployment Rate Currently)
dz - dc	=	Change in the difference in unemployment between EZs and their surrounding communities

zones and their surrounding communities is significant with a probability value of .0006. Thus, the first directional hypothesis on Unemployment Impact is confirmed. The difference of means for the zone is 3.8% and the surrounding community is 2.3%, while the change in the difference of means is 1.5%. Again, the difference in the zone is about 65% greater than the difference in the surrounding community, which makes the significance level appear to be predictable before confirming it with the T-test.

This statistically significant decrease in EZ unemployment is the most important contribution of this study to the field of public policy research. Therefore, this analysis shows that EZs do have a positive impact on reducing unemployment. This positive impact is especially meaningful, since, historically, poverty areas are the last to improve in good economic times and the first to get worse in bad economic times. Again, this significant unemployment outcome is the foundation and dependent variable for testing the impacts between the EZs in the remaining hypotheses. (Additionally, the single case study in Part Two supports the conclusion of a positive employment impact. In Portland, Oregon 61% of all new hires are zone residents.)

CAUSAL IMPACTS BETWEEN ZONES

As discussed in chapter three, the remaining hypotheses are analyzed by first utilizing simple regression analysis, T-tests, analysis of variance (ANOVA), and a correlation matrix to establish the significant building blocks for the more sophisticated techniques of multiple regression stepwise and residual analyses. This provides a very strong methodology for testing the variables and hypotheses.

SIMPLE REGRESSION

The next step in testing the remaining hypotheses is taken by using a simple regression technique for measuring the significance of each independent variable with interval and ratio data. Thus, hypotheses 2, 3, 5, 6, and 7 are tested, with the independent variables of Time, Number of Incentives, Land Use, Population Density, and Geographic Size respectively.

The simple regression results show significance only for one of the independent variables with either interval or ratio data, the Period of Time (in Months). Thus, Time or Months is the only variable in this first set that will be used in the upcoming higher analysis of the multiple regression stepwise technique. In reviewing a graph on the slope on the Number of Incentives, there is an indication with a gradual upward slope that significance could result if this variable is divided into groups. But measuring the regression coefficient of this data by dividing it into three interval groups does not produce significance, so the quantity of incentives are recoded into high and low dichotomous groups to test for the difference of means with a T-test.

T-TESTS

As noted earlier, a T-test with paired groups was utilized to measure the significance level for hypothesis 1 on Unemployment Impact. Subsequently, T-tests with independent groups are used to measure the significance levels for hypothesis 3 on the Number of Incentives and hypothesis 4 on the Kind of Incentives. Table VII on page 89 shows the four T-tests for the single and combined incentive variables, with the top illustrating the high/low Rank, the second and third illustrating the two types of incentives, *employer* Property Tax abatements and *employer* Income Tax credits, and the bottom illustrating Property Tax and Income Tax combined. Rank is signficant. Also, Property Tax (individually), and Property Tax and Income Tax combined, are the only incentives out of the twelve different types of incentives that are significant. The lists and descriptions showing the states and types of incentives in the study by Erickson and Friedman (1991) and the summary by HUD (1992) were utilized to create the data for the independent variables in testing hypothesis 4 on the Kind of Incentives.

As discussed in the last chapter, the high Rank was from five to eight incentives and the low Rank was from one to four incentives. The high group has a 1.72% greater impact on unemployment than the low group, and is significant at the .023 level. This outcome is a positive indicator in reducing EZ unemployment, but it is not necessarily a strong indicator since the incentives as fixed and equal intervals, and scaled from one to eight, are not significant. This outcome does not take into

TABLE VII

T-TESTS

Independent Variables (Incentives)	N	Mean	Standard Deviation
RANK:			
High	36	2.16	3.4
Low	24	0.44	2.3
Difference		1.72	0.8
p = .023			
PROPERTY TAX:			
Yes	47	2.04	3.2
No	13	-0.62	1.7
Difference		2.66	0.9
p = .0003			
INCOME TAX:			
Yes	44	1.90	3.2
No	16	0.27	2.8
Difference		1.63	0.9
p = .0617			
COMBINED PROPERTY AND INCOME TAXES:			
Both	33	2.65	3.2
One or neither	27	.02	2.3
		2.63	0.7
p = .0005			

Dependent Variable = d_z - d_c (or the change in the difference in unemployment between EZs and their surrounding communities)

Property and Income Tax incentives are for the "employer"

N = number of cases

account the different revenue amounts or dollar values that separate states have for specific incentives. Thus, there is no qualitative value on the amount of each incentive between the states, only the quantitative number of incentives is analyzed in this test. Up to this point in time, no study has provided the measurable amount of value for each type of incentive between the states, and to do so is another recommendation by the author for further study by EZ researchers.

The next three T-tests on Table VII provide means and significance levels for the two variables, Property Tax and Income Tax, in regard to the Kind of Incentives. Between zones with and without these incentives, Property Tax abatements have a 2.66% greater impact on unemployment at a significance level of .0003, Income Tax credits have a 1.63% greater impact on unemployment at a significance level of .0617, and Property Tax abatements and Income Tax credits combined have a 2.63% greater impact on unemployment at a significance level of .0005.. In fact, those zones without Property Tax incentives have a -0.62 or negative impact on unemployment. This outcome shows these incentives to be strong indicators of EZ performance. Although, Income Tax incentives alone are not quite significant, they are significant in combination with Property Tax incentives. (Property Tax and Income Tax combined will be specifically investigated in the next section or ANOVA.) Income Tax incentives are relevant to the predictive model, since they are significant in combination and their individualized impact on unemployment of 1.63% is greater than the average of 1.5%. Again, Property Tax incentives, and Property Tax and Income Tax incentives combined have a significant and much greater impact on reducing unemployment than the average zone with 2.66% and 2.63% positive impacts respectively.

ANALYSIS OF VARIANCE

The separate and combined impacts on unemployment of the two incentives, Property Tax and Income Tax, were evaluated with an ANOVA illustrated in Table VIII on page 91. ANOVA is used to measure the means only and is not used as a test for correlation and statistical significance between the two independent variables. The mean square value (F-test) translated into a probability value (neither value is shown in Table VIII to prevent confusion) indicates that there is no interaction or

TABLE VIII

ANALYSIS OF VARIANCE

TAX INCENTIVES: INDEPENDENT VARIABLES

Property	Income	N	Mean	Standard Deviation
No	No	2	-2.10	2.97
No	Yes	11	-0.35	1.47
Yes	No	14	0.61	2.67
Yes	Yes	33	2.65	3.22

Dependent Variable = d_z - d_c (or the change in the difference in unemployment between EZs and their surrounding communities)

N = number of cases

linkage between the two incentives. These variables have no influence on each other, but the earlier T-tests show the significance of these variables in reducing unemployment.

The important point in Table VIII is that those zones with both Property Tax and Income Tax incentives *combined* have a 2.65% greater impact on unemployment, while those zones with neither or single incentives have either a negative or a minimal impact on unemployment. This indicates a major impact on reducing unemployment when Property Tax and Income Tax incentives are both utilized in tandem, although Property Tax is the strongest of the two incentives. All of these ANVOA outcomes intensify the interpretive meaning that the two combined incentives have a major impact on reducing unemployment. Thus, the ANOVA supports the inclusion of Income Tax in the subsequent predictive analyses.

CORRELATION MATRIX

After completing the T-tests and initial simple regression analysis, there are three independent variables that have shown statistical significance and one independent variable that has shown conceptual relevance, which are tested by the more sophisticated regression and residual methods. Before these advanced techniques are utilized, the variables are analyzed by utilizing the correlation matrix in Table IX on page 93, which provides the Pearson's correlation coefficients and simple regression probability values. Again, Unemployment Impact or dz-dc (change in the difference in unemployment between EZs and their surrounding communities) is the dependent variable for further analysis. Rank and Property Tax are significant independent variables as measured by the T-tests. Months is a significant independent variable as measured by the simple regression analysis. Income Tax is a significant independent variable when combined with Property Tax in the T-test. Also, Income Tax is relevant by its greater than average impact on unemployment as a single variable in the T-test, and its much greater than average impact on unemployment when combined with Property Tax in the ANOVA.

The correlation with the Unemployment Impact is strongest by the incentive variable of Property Tax (.36), followed by Months (.31), Rank (.27) and Income Tax

TABLE IX

CORRELATION MATRIX

PEARSON'S CORRELATION COEFFICIENTS:

	Unemployment Impact (dz-dc)	Property Tax	Months (time)	Rank (high/low)	Income Tax
Unemployment Impact*	1.00 .00	.36 .0054	.31 .0171	.27 .0352	.23 .0732
Property Tax	.36	1.00	-.01	.23	-.13
Months (time)	.31	-.01	1.00	.20	.48
Rank (high/low)	.27	.23	.20	1.00	.66
Income Tax	.23	-.13	.48	.66	1.00

* *Unemployment Impact or (dz - dc) = dependent variable. Pearson's correlation coefficient = top score. Simple regression probability value = bottom score.*

Key to Table IX

dz - dc   = Change in the difference in unemployment between EZs and their surrounding communities

(.23). Between independent variables, there is a very strong correlation by Income Tax with Rank (.66) and Months (.48) respectively. This very strong correlation indicates that Income Tax has a broad overlapping influence with Months and Rank on Unemployment Impact, which would reduce the predictive correlation for the weaker variables in the forthcoming multiple regression stepwise technique.

It was anticipated that both Income Tax and Property Tax would have a strong correlation with Rank, since Rank divides the Number of Incentives into two groups, those with many incentives and those with few incentives. Yet, according to the correlation, those zones with a Property Tax incentive are not conglomerated into the high group, as are those zones that have an Income Tax incentive. Thus, Property Tax does not have a broad overlapping influence with Rank, as does Income Tax with both Rank and Months. So, Property Tax should maintain its individual strength as an indicator of Unemployment Impact and it should be the strongest indicator in the forthcoming sophisticated regression method. Another important point is that there are no other strong correlations in the matrix, and this is especially true for Property Tax and Months, and Property Tax and Income Tax, which have no correlations and very slight inverse correlations with -.01 and -.13 coefficients respectively.

Lastly, the simple regression probability values in the correlation matrix reiterate the link of the significant and relevant independent variables with the dependent variable. These significant values determine the selection of variables that are utilized in the advanced predictive method in the next section. The probability value for Months is the same as was tested earlier, while the values for Property Tax, Income Tax, and Rank are slightly varied from the values in the T-tests. This is explained by the fact that the earlier T-tests appropriately reported values based on "separate variances" (where it is assumed that the variances between the two groups of the independent variable are *not* the same), and not the "pooled variances" (where it is assumed that the variances between the two groups of the independent variable *are* the same). The values for the pooled variances and the simple regression in the correlation matrix are mathematically identical, however, both values for the separate and pooled variances are significant.

MULTIPLE REGRESSION STEPWISE ANALYSIS

After completing the previous analytical building blocks, a sophisticated predictive model with the influences on the dependent variable (Unemployment Impact) by the significant and revelant independent variables (Property Tax, Months, Rank, and Income Tax) is investigated with the multiple regression stepwise technique. On pages 96-97, Table X illustrates the final step summary with the components of a regression model, and a step-by-step explanation of the variance with the influences of each independent variable. Each independent variable is entered according to the level of correlation with the dependent variable as previously shown in the correlation matrix.

The total R-square or variance explained is nearly 24.7%, and the multiple regression's final step is significant at a level of .0032. Property Tax has the strongest influence in the regression model, followed by Months and Income Tax, and lastly by Rank, according to the standardized Beta weight. Due to the multicollinearity between Income Tax and Months, and Income Tax and Rank, these variables adjusted in each step in the degree of influence or amount of regression weight.

In the final step, Property Tax is the only variable that is significant (with b at least twice as high as the standard error), since the multicollinearity changed the significance levels for Income Tax, Months, and Rank variables (although each of these variables is significant when excluding the other multicollinear variables). Also, Rank has the least influence of all the variables and has very little variance explained, due to the fact that the other variables are stronger indicators or predictors. However, Rank is an important indicator when calculating predictions on Unemployment Impact with the regression model. The predictive findings and far-reaching conclusions of the regression model will be discussed in the next chapter.

Finally, the step-by-step summary shows that the Prperty Tax and Months explain most of the variance at over 22%, with Income Tax contributing another 2% to the overall total. However, when Months is excluded from the model, Income Tax

TABLE X

MULTIPLE REGRESSION STEPWISE ANALYSIS

FINAL STEP SUMMARY:

Dependent Variable   = *Unemployment Impact (dz - dc)*

R-Square   = *.2472*

Probability Value   = *.0032*

Independent Variables	b	Beta	Standard Error
Property Tax (PT)	2.72	.36	0.99
Months (MO)	0.03	.24	0.02
Income Tax (IT)	0.92	.13	1.36
Rank (RK)	0.35	.06	1.12
Constant	-3.18	---	1.42

Regression Model of b:
Unemployment impact (dz - dc) = Constant + PT + MO + IT + RK or
-3.18 + 2.72 x (PT 0 or 1) + .03 x (MO 1-71) + .92 x (IT 0 or 1) + .35 x (RK 1 or 2)
(Formula is rounded off to a hundredth.)

STEP-BY-STEP SUMMARY:

Variables Entered	R-Square	R-Square Change	Percent Change
1. Property Tax	.1259	.1259	12.6
2. Months	.2226	.0967	9.7
3. Income Tax	.2458	.0232	2.3
4. Rank	.2472	.0014	0.1

TABLE X continued

Key Table X

dz - dc	=	*The change in the difference in unemployment between EZs and their surrounding communities.*
R-Squared	=	*The proportion of variance explained in the dependent variable by the independent variables.*
Probability Value	=	*Statistical significance level (.05 or below is significant).*
Constant	=	*Intercept a or the value of the dependent variable when the independent variables are equal to zero.*
b	=	*The partial regression coefficient or the change produced in the dependent variable by a unit change in the independent variables controlling for the other independent variables.*
Beta	=	*The partial "standardized" regression coefficient or the change produced in the dependent variable by a unit change in the independent variable when both are measured in terms of standard deviation units.*
Standard Error	=	*A measure of the standard deviation of b values where b should be two times the standard error to reject the null hypothesis.*

and Rank nearly make up all of the variance explained by Months.

SUMMARIZING THE REMAINING HYPOTHESES

As discussed in Chapter III, hypotheses 2 through 7 test for the different impacts on unemployment between the EZs. Three of these hypotheses (on Time, and Number and Kind of Incentives) have been confirmed through the statistical analyses, and all six of the remaining hypotheses will be summarized in the following discussion.

Hypothesis 2. The change in the difference in unemployment between EZs and their surrounding communities is proportional to the period of time since EZ designation.

The second hypothesis on time has been confirmed and the variable was created in Months instead of years, so that a continuum of expanded interval data could be better utilized in the analyses. The Months variable is significant. It was originally conceived in the research design that the length of time would be a very strong indicator on the impact of unemployment when comparing the EZs. Time has proven to be so.

Hypothesis 3. The change in the difference in unemployment between EZs and their surrounding communities is proportional to the number of EZ incentives.

The Number of Incentives placed into two dichotomous groups does confirm the third hypothesis. Rank is significant, but it is not necessarily a strong indicator, since the number of incentives utilized as interval data from one to eight is not significant. Since there is no qualitative measurement on the value or strength of each incentive between the states, the grouping is only a significant indicator of Unemployment Impact for states with either many (5-8) or few (1-4) incentives. Yet, this high versus low incentive package is an important indicator in the predictive model.

Hypothesis 4. The change in the difference in unemployment between EZs and their surrounding communities is proportional to the kind of incentives.

There are two types of incentives that confirm the fourth hypothesis, as employer Property Tax abatements (individually or combined with Income Tax) and employer Income Tax credits (when combined with Property Tax) are significant. These two incentives are strong indicators on Unemployment Impact. (The single case study in Part Two, Chapter VII, supports the conclusion that Property Tax abatements have a positive impact on the employment of zone residents.) Property Tax is individually strong, while Income Tax is highly correlated with both Months and Rank. Overall, the Property Tax type of incentive variable has a very strong influence in the regression model, and this appears to be due to the dollar value available to the employers from this incentive, as shown in the U.S. Department of Housing and Urban Development summary (1992). Thus, there appears to be a correlation between the "dollar value" of the incentive with the "type" of incentive, which needs to be studied further.

It is important to note that these variables are "employer-based incentives," and their influence is in accord with the theoretical premise that incentives for employers are the most effective in creating and retaining jobs. Additionally, the Sales Tax variable by itself was not significant in this study, but there is some indication that it is significant within a full-scale incentives package. Also other economic impact studies show that the level of sales taxes is an important indicator to business activity and job growth. Thus, the Sales Tax incentive should be investigated in future studies.

Hypothesis 5. The change in the difference in unemployment between EZs and their surrounding communities is proportional to variations in EZ land use (i.e., percentages of residential, commercial, industrial, open space, and other).

The fifth hypothesis is disconfirmed, since none of the Land Use combinations are significant. This indicates that EZs effectively reduce unemployment regardless of the variations of land development. This also indicates that it is the incentives within the EZ areas, and not the land development, which is the primary influence on reducing unemployment. This finding is somewhat contrary to that of a previous study by Erickson, Friedman, and McCluskey (1989), which found that EZs in primarily manufacturing areas produce more jobs than the EZs in other areas. However, this study did not compare study and control groups. So, it is recommended that the variations in EZ land development should again be analyzed in future studies.

Hypothesis 6. The change in the difference in unemployment between EZs and their surrounding communities is proportional to EZ population density.

The sixth hypothesis is disconfirmed, as the Population variable is not significant. This indicates that EZs effectively reduce unemployment regardless of the Population densities in both urban and rural EZ areas. Thus, urban EZ residents and rural EZ residents are both benefitting from EZs in their communities.

Hypothesis 7. The change in the difference in unemployment between EZs and their surrounding communities is proportional to EZ geographic size.

The seventh hypothesis is disconfirmed, as the Square Miles variable is not significant. This indicates that EZs effectively reduce unemployment regardless of the boundary or size, as long as the EZ program is specifically targeted within the study's data set with a boundary range of .4 to 44 square miles. This does not translate into making predictions, either pro or con, on broader or regional areas with economic development programs.

It should also be noted that the variables from the three disconfirmed hypotheses are correlated, and therefore, are not significant (collectively as well as individually) when testing for their combinations of influence. Residential, Commercial, and Industrial land development variables are intercorrelated with the more dense Populations and smaller boundary Size variables of urban areas. Open and Other land development variables are intercorrelated with the less dense Population and larger boundary Size variables of rural areas. By definition, EZs target depressed and multifarious business districts, so it is not surprising that there would be job growth in most of these urban and rural areas, regardless of their descriptive characteristics, when strong economic incentives have been in place for considerable lengths of time.

In sum, the first hypothesis (on Unemployment Impact) is confirmed and is the foundation of this study. The second, third, and fourth hypotheses (on Time, and Number and Kind of Incentives) are confirmed, and their significant variables explain 24.7% of the variance on the differences between the EZs. Since only a quarter or so of the variance is explained, there are other influences to be considered. But the fifth, sixth, and seventh hypotheses (on Land Use, Population, and Size) are disconfirmed, and their variables are neither significant nor do they contribute to the predictive model on the differences between the EZs. However, the findings on all of the hypotheses provide valuable information on gaining a greater understanding of EZs.

CHAPTER VI

POLICY IMPLICATIONS AND CONCLUSIONS

PREDICTIVE FINDINGS

After confirming several hypotheses, the significant variables (Unemployment Impact, Property Tax, Months, Income Tax, and Rank) are manipulated into the predictive model. The first section is a *specific* application of the regression model, which produces specific residuals for each EZ case (actual versus predicted) within the study's data set. The second section is a *general* application of the regression model, which produces predictive findings applicable to all EZ programs in general-- past, present and future. However, other external influences are unaccounted for in the linear models, such as the effects of a shrinking number of unemployed workers, so this fact should temper any interpretations of the predictive findings, especially for the generalized model.

RESIDUAL ANALYSIS

The regression model is specifically applied to each EZ case in the study with the residual analysis in Table XI on pages 104-106. The residual analysis utilizes the regression formula on all of the significant independent variables (Property Tax, Months, Income Tax, and Rank) in calculating the predicted values for the dependent variable (Unemployment Impact) for each EZ case. Then a comparison between the *actual* Unemployment Impact by each EZ versus the *predicted* Unemployment Impact by each EZ, forms the residual or margin of error. There are many EZs that perform

TABLE XI

RESIDUAL ANALYSIS

State/Zone	PT	MO	IT	RK	Actual	Predicted*	Residual
ALABAMA:							
Dallas Co.	0	24	0	1	-4.2	-2.02	-2.18
CALIFORNIA:							
Fresno	0	32	1	2	-3.9	-0.49	-3.41
Pittsburgh	0	17	1	2	0.0	-0.99	0.99
FLORIDA:							
Franklin	1	29	0	2	0.0	1.21	-1.21
ILLINOIS:							
Belleville	1	47	1	2	0.3	2.74	-2.44
Belvider	1	47	1	2	0.6	2.74	-2.14
Blue Island	1	47	1	2	0.0	2.74	-2.74
Bureau	1	23	1	2	0.4	1.93	-1.53
Centralia	1	23	1	2	0.0	1.93	-1.93
Danville	1	59	1	2	4.7	3.14	1.56
Dixon	-1	23	1	2	-0.7	1.93	-2.63
East Chicago	1	5	1	2	0.0	1.32	-1.32
Illiopolis	1	35	1	2	0.0	2.33	-2.33
Mound City	1	60	1	2	0.0	3.18	-3.18
Olney	1	23	1	2	9.6	1.93	7.67
Riverbend	1	36	1	2	-0.6	2.37	-2.97
Rock Island	1	47	1	2	6.2	2.74	3.46
SW Madison	1	47	1	2	0.6	2.74	-2.14
Urbana	1	47	1	2	1.4	2.74	-1.34
Will Co.	1	71	1	2	7.8	3.55	4.25
INDIANA:							
Anderson	1	65	1	2	9.3	3.35	5.95
Elkhart	1	53	1	2	1.6	2.94	-1.34
Evansville	1	65	1	2	6.7	3.35	3.35
Hammond	1	50	1	2	1.0	2.84	-1.84
Madison	1	53	1	2	4.0	2.94	1.06
Michigan	1	65	1	2	3.5	3.35	0.15
KENTUCKY:							
Ashland	1	64	1	1	1.7	2.97	-1.27
Campbell	1	31	1	1	0.6	1.85	-1.25
Covington	1	64	1	1	1.4	2.97	-1.57

TABLE XI continued

RESIDUAL ANALYSIS

State/Zone	PT	MO	IT	RK	Actual	Predicted*	Residual
MISSOURI:							
Brookfield	1	64	1	2	5.4	3.31	2.09
Chillicothe	1	56	1	2	-2.8	3.04	-5.84
St. Joseph	1	49	1	2	3.9	2.81	1.09
NEVADA:							
Las Vegas	0	5	0	1	0.0	-2.67	2.67
NEW JERSEY:							
Camden	0	31	1	2	0.6	-0.52	1.12
Millville	0	39	1	2	-0.6	-0.25	-0.35
Orange City	0	29	1	2	-2.3	-0.59	-1.71
OHIO:							
Ashland	1	31	1	2	2.0	2.20	-0.20
Columbus	1	48	1	2	3.3	2.77	0.53
Fairfield	1	52	1	2	9.6	2.91	6.69
Marion Co.	1	7	1	2	2.7	1.39	1.31
Springfield	1	26	1	2	3.3	2.03	1.27
OREGON:							
Seaside	1	6	0	1	0.0	0.09	-0.09
PENN-SYLVANIA:							
Johnstown	1	69	0	1	-3.0	2.21	-5.21
Lancaster	1	69	0	1	6.3	2.21	4.09
McKeesport	1	57	0	1	-0.1	1.81	-1.91
Monessen	1	8	0	1	-3.0	0.16	-3.16
Reading	1	29	0	1	1.0	0.86	0.14
TEXAS:							
Athens	1	9	0	1	0.0	0.19	-0.19
Brownsville	1	9	0	1	1.0	0.19	0.81
Dimmett	1	3	0	1	0.0	-0.01	0.01
Gainsville	1	7	0	1	0.0	0.12	-0.12
Mount Pleasant	1	4	0	1	0.2	-0.02	0.18
San Benito	1	1	0	1	0.0	-0.08	0.08
Texas City	1	1	0	1	6.2	0.12	6.08

TABLE XI continued

RESIDUAL ANALYSIS

State/Zone	PT	MO	IT	RK	Actual	Predicted*	Residual
VIRGINIA:							
Chesapeake	0	49	1	1	0.5	-0.26	0.76
Danville	0	65	1	1	0.0	0.28	-0.28
Newport	0	65	1	1	0.7	0.28	0.42
Norfolk	0	65	1	1	0.9	0.28	0.62
Saltville	0	65	1	1	0.0	0.28	-0.28
Waynesboro	0	17	1	1	0.3	-1.34	1.64

* *Regression Model of b:*
Unemployment Impact (dz - dc) = Constant + PT + MO + IT + RK or
-3.18 + 2.72 x (PT 0 or 1) + .03 x (MO 1-71) + .92 x (IT 0 or 1) + .35 x (RK 1 or 2)
(Formula is rounded off to a hundredth.)

Key to Table XII

PT	=	Property tax incentive (0 = no, 1 = yes)
MO	=	Months (period of time)
IT	=	Income tax incentive (0 = no, 1 = yes)
RK	=	Rank (1 = low group or 1-4 incentives, 2 = high group or 5-8 incentives)
Actual	=	Actual unemployment impact by zone (dz - dc or the change in the difference in unemployment between EZs and their surrounding communities)
Predicted	=	Predicted unemployment impact by zone based on regression model
Residual	=	Margin of "error" between actual and predicted
b	=	The partial regression coefficient or the change produced in the dependent variable by a unit change in the independent variable controlling for the other independent variables

according to the predictive model, while many others perform contrary to the predictive model with plus or minus margins of error. This shows a varied mix of performances by the EZs and states.

There is little residual or error for Texas and Virginia, but both have few incentives. Texas has been active with EZs for less than a year, with a Property Tax incentive and without an Income Tax incentive, and the performance is in accord with the predictive model, except for one EZ (Texas City). Conversely, Virginia has been active for several years, with an Income Tax incentive and without a Property Tax incentive, and the performance is also in accord with the predictive model. Thus, Texas and Virginia conform to the predictive model more so than the other states.

Illinois has the most EZs, which perform strongly in both directions with plus and minus residuals, and two EZs (Olney and Will County) perform much better than what the model predicts. Also, Indiana has one EZ (Anderson), Missouri has one EZ (Chillicothe), Ohio has one EZ (Fairfield), Pennsylvania has one EZ (Lancaster), and again Texas has one EZ (Texas City) which performed much better than what the model predicts. All of these EZs perform 4-6% better than what the model predicts. Illinois, Indiana, Missouri, and Ohio all have full-scale incentive packages, so it is not surprising that these states would have some EZs that perform exceptionally well.

Contrariwise, Missouri has one EZ (Chillicothe) and Pennsylvania has one EZ (Johnstown), which perform over 5% worse than what the model predicts. All of the EZs in Alabama, Florida, and Kentucky perform worse than what the model predicts, which include much of the southern region. Additionally, Alabama, California, Nevada, and New Jersey (in a cross-section of regions) are all predicted to have a *negative* performance. This is due to the fact that these states have weak incentives, and do not have "combined" employer Property Tax abatements and employer Income Tax credits, which are the strongest influences of all the incentives on Unemployment Impact. As predicted, the EZs in Alabama, California, Nevada, and New Jersey perform poorly on reducing unemployment. This is in accord with the theoretical precise that poverty areas are the first to get worse in bad economic times and the last to get better in good economic times, especially when there are no strong economic incentives in the poverty areas.

As a policy-making tool, the residual analysis provides all states with measurable and specific feedback on performance, which can assist the states in changing their legislated policies and incentives on poorly performing EZ programs. Also, the regression model can help to effectively create and implement new EZ programs and policies by the states and federal government.

PREDICTIVE MODEL

The full-scale incentive package (with Property Tax, Income Tax, and High Rank) is manipulated into the regression model in Table XII on page 109 to illustrate the predictive values (between Unemployment Impact and Months). This is translated into an impact/time series table, which shows the number of Months that it takes for an incentive package to cause a specific percentage of Unemployment Impact. This predictive model can universally be applied to creating EZ policies and programs, but the linear estimates should not be concluded as precise for the relationship between large amounts of Time and large changes in Unemployment Impact.

An Unemployment Impact of 1.5%, which is the average per zone/community in the study, is a good indicator for comparing the various incentive packages. A full-scale incentive package of Property Tax, Income Tax, and High Rank, shows an average Unemployment Impact in 10 months or under a year. This finding illustrates the immediate impact that a full-scale EZ program has on reducing unemployment. When Property Tax and Income Tax are combined with Low Rank, the average Unemployment Impact occurs in 20 months or under two years. When Property Tax and High Rank are combined, the average Unemployment Impact occurs in 37 months or over 3 years. These incentive packages have a strong influence, which are quicker than the average in the study's data set with a mean of 38 months.

Property Tax is a predictor in every equation where the average Unemployment Impact occurs within the 71 month range of the study's data set. When reviewing the relative strength of the variables between the states in the U.S. Department of Housing and Urban Development summary (1992), Property Tax appears to have much more relative value in dollars than the other incentives. This

TABLE XII

REGRESSION MODEL

Regression Model of b:
Unemployment Impact (dz - dc) = Constant + PT + MO + IT + RK
or -3.18 + 2.72 x (PT 0 or 1) + .03 x (MO 1-71) + .92 x (IT 0 or 1) + .35 x (RK 1 or 2)
(Formula is rounded off to a hundredth.)

R-Square or variance explained = 24.7%

dz - dc	*# Months**	*State/Local Incentive Package*
1.5%	*10*	*Property and Income Taxes, and High Rank*
1.5%	*20*	*Property and Income Taxes, and Low Rank*
1.5%	*37*	*Property Tax and High Rank*
1.5%	*47*	*Property Tax and Low Rank*
1.5%	*90*	*Income Tax and High Rank*
1.5%	*101*	*Income Tax and Low Rank*
1.5%	*118*	*High Rank*
1.5%	*128*	*Low Rank*
6.0%	*143*	*Property and Income Taxes, and High Rank*

* The number of months is strictly a linear estimate.

Key to Table XII

dz - dc at 1.5%	=	*This unemployment impact is the average of the study's data set*
dz - dc at 6.0%	=	*This unemployment impact would result in the average EZ being equal to its surrounding community*
R-Square	=	*The proportion of variance explained in the dependent variable by the independent variables*
PT	=	*Property Tax incentive (0 = no, 1 = yes)*
IT	=	*Income Tax incentive (0 = no, 1 = yes)*
MO	=	*Months (range = 1-71)*
RK	=	*Rank (1 = low group or 1-4 incentives, 2 = high group or 5-8 incentives)*
b	=	*The partial regression coefficient or the change produced in the dependent variable by a unit change in the independent variable controlling for the other independent variables*

accounts for Property Tax having the single most influence on Unemployment Impact. Income Tax and High Rank are also important predictors in reducing the length of time for having an impact on unemployment. Low Rank has the least influence on reducing the length of time. One or the other Rank groupings must be included in every equation, since a Low Rank means that there is at least one incentive, but no more than four incentives. By definition, Property Tax and Income Tax must include some influence by Rank in the equation, especially since this low/high criterion is included in the interaction of all the regression weights.

An Unemployment Impact of 6%, which causes the average EZ to be equal to its surrounding community, is illustrated with a full-scale incentive package. An average Unemployment Impact of 6% will occur in 143 months or nearly 12 years. Generally speaking, this means that a full-scale EZ program could be designed by any state with a policy goal of reducing unemployment in the EZ to the level of its surrounding community in ten and a half years. This also means that a full-scale EZ program at the state level is a long term program, but with a significant impact on unemployment in just three months as noted in Table XII. A substantive federal program could also add a greater and quicker impact on unemployment, which will be discussed in the next section.

Finally, all of the above findings on the amounts of Time and changes of Unemployment Impact are based strictly on linear estimates, which exclude any other factors. This has limitations. For instance, due to the shrinking inventory of unemployed workers, it takes more and more time to close the unemployment rate gap between EZs and their surrounding communities, as the percentage of the gap shrinks. It should be noted that findings based on linear estimates should not be regarded as precise conclusions, but only as directional trends. However, the results and predictive model do show relative "thresholds," where a small-scale incentives package has little impact, while a large-scale incentives package has a significant impact (over time) on employment.

POLICY RECOMMENDATIONS

There are many policy recommendations that have been inferred and referred to throughout this study, and these will be reviewed in the three following categories and summaries:

INCENTIVES

It is highly recommended that both the federal and state governments should implement *substantive* EZ incentives and legislation. This recommendation is based on the fact the EZs with full-scale incentives do have a major impact on reducing unemployment. Some states have already implemented substantive EZs, however, many states could improve and revise their EZ legislation, while other states should create EZ legislation.

The influence of an EZ incentive is related to its dollar value, although the influence and not the relative dollar value (which varies between the states for the same type of incentive) was analyzed in this study. Within existing state programs, the influence of employer property tax abatements is the strongest of the state/local incentives, which makes property tax incentives the most influential factor in reducing unemployment, especially when they are combined with employer income tax credits. Consequently, the influence of employer income tax credits is also strong when combined with the employer property tax abatements. Thus, states should either add or create these combined incentives for EZs in implementing a full-scale program at the state/local level.

The federal government should increase the economic incentives in its EZ legislation, but the newest bill may or may not be of any help to significantly strengthening the nine federal/state EZs (yet to be designated) with the supplemental economic incentives. The new bill adds an employer income tax credit at the federal level, and this type of incentive proved to be a significant variable in reducing unemployment in this study, but only when combined with a property tax abatement. Thus, the federal incentive will only be significant for those EZs that already have existing property tax abatements. Additionally, the federal income tax credit for EZ employers has a dollar value larger than the income tax credits in the states, but it is also restricted to the hiring of zone residents, whereas many states target incentives for employers to the hiring of new employees in general.

Relatively speaking, the dollar value of employer income tax credits is not nearly as strong as the capital gains tax exclusions for employers in the previously proposed federal legislation. The dollar value of capital gains tax exclusions at the federal level is even stronger than the property tax abatements at the state/local level, so the capital gains tax incentive has the greatest potential of all incentives for reducing unemployment. Historically, lowering the capital gains tax rate has spurred massive investment in general (Brookes 1982), as capital is the life-blood of investment. As this study strongly indicates by translating the state experience to the federal level, amending the new bill by mandating a full-scale incentives package, such as adding capital gains tax exclusions, is necessary for a serious and ambitious EZ program at the federal level.

Reducing interest rates and regulatory burdens on loans for EZ firms is another moderate step that should be taken for increasing incentives. Community development banks and funds would not only be an impetus to start-up and expanding businesses, but these financial institutions could serve as a fingerpost and marketing tool for encouraging investment in EZs. Financial banking incentives also have the advantage of weighing the "risks" of participating businesses.

Incentives should primarily be targeted at employers, which is where jobs are created and entrepreneurship is formulated. The results of this study confirms that incentives for employers are the only significant variables in reducing unemployment. However, supplemental incentives for residents and employees, such as personal income tax deductions and health insurance credits, should be implemented as additional building blocks to a full-scale incentives package. Also, infrastructure maintenance and redevelopment should be included in any community development policy and financed by increased EZ tax revenues (as is done in New Jersey).

ADMINISTRATION, JURISDICTION, AND SCOPE

It is recommended that EZs should be a *combined* federal and state/local government initiative wherever possible. It is not possible that the federal government can match every state EZ area, which totals over 3,000 in number and is growing, although a combined approach for selected EZs should have the most effective means in reducing unemployment by providing a greater incentives package. A federal effort should be as expansive in scope as possible, while targeting the poverty areas with the severest needs. Thus, the new bill should be amended to designate many more areas than merely nine for receiving incentives (as well as providing much greater economic incentives).

However, any federal regulation should not stifle local control. So, the new bill should be amended to allow for greater state/local autonomy in experimenting with new initiatives. An excellent example of this type of federalism, cooperation, and innovation is the allowance of a federal welfare waiver in regard to the State of Wisconsin's workfare program in two counties. Removing the distance between citizens and programs by fostering a *localized* cooperative partnership is essential to the efficiency and efficacy of the targeted EZ program. Thus, local control is central to local policy initiatives.

The federal and state governments should mandate that annual and specific unemployment data be reported on EZs and their surrounding communities. This administrative report should be a necessary regulation for designation. This report on unemployment is vital in evaluating the effectiveness of an EZ program, and to the making of new and improved EZ policies where necessary.

EZs need to be better marketed. A stipulation upon designation should also be that there is an administrative marketing plan to strategically assist in producing an effective EZ program. The Illinois and Maryland studies show that many business owners and managers do not know about the incentives, even when these businesses are located in designated EZ areas. Advertising, communication, and information should be essential components of every administered EZ program.

However, other regulations and red tape should be reduced, since an Illinois study showed that many firms do not apply for incentives due to the excessive paper work and cumbersome administrative process. Regulatory relief should be a priority in all aspects of economic development. Regulatory relief, in general, is a stimulus to business, especially small business, as it causes fewer impediments to starting a business and fewer costs to staying in business. Regulatory relief will increase the effectiveness of an EZ program.

RESEARCH

It is recommended that several more scholarly investigations are needed to evaluate the results of EZs. EZ job creation and retention, along with EZ business creation and retention, should be continuously studied. The data is currently too limited to do thorough analyses in these areas. As time moves on, more and more data should become available for extensive studies.

More benefit-cost analyses should be completed, especially on the costs per EZ job created, plus the benefits per EZ business created or expanded. This should include the reduction of welfare assistance and the addition of tax revenues generated by EZ employers and employees, directly and indirectly, as well as spillover effects in the surrounding communities. More benefit-cost analyses would also provide valuable information on the thresholds (lower and higher) of incentive packages.

A study on the relative strengths and dollar values of the incentives is greatly needed, so that the influences of the same and varying incentives between the states can be thoroughly evaluated. The strength of an incentive is related to its dollar value, but a scale is necessary to compare the same types of incentives with differing dollar values between the states.

More study is needed on the impact of sales taxes, not only for retail businesses but for industrial businesses, which make large purchases of equipment and supplies for production, especially in those states with high sales tax rates. Although EZ programs are varied between the states, there are common and major components amongst many states and localities, such as income, property, and sales tax incentives, which are worthy of further analysis. As noted earlier, only property and income taxes by themselves have significant impacts on reducing unemployment in this study. However, there are indications in this study that sales tax incentives are significant within a full-scale package of incentives. There may also be some EZs where sales taxes alone are significant.

The impact of land use and development should be studied further, as the results of this study were in partial contrast to those on manufacturing areas in an earlier study. This can be explained by the fact that the earlier study only counted the number of EZ jobs created without comparing study and control groups. However, more analyses on land use and development is in order.

More study on EZ businesses (kinds of industries, and sizes of companies, and increases, changes or shifts in any participating corporation's EZ and non-EZ production sites) and on the impacts of financial incentives would be helpful on evaluating EZs. Also, more study on the comparison between the "jobs to people" (targeting geography) approach versus the "people to jobs" (targeting portability) approach is needed.

Lastly, the specific impacts on EZ residents should be studied further. In Part Two, the author is attempting to take the first step forward by analyzing the total EZ jobs created versus the EZ jobs created and filled by EZ residents in Portland, Oregon. This constitutes a landmark case study on the new jobs and zone resident.

SUMMARY STATEMENT

In conclusion, this study has shown that EZs are very effective in reducing unemployment, and that the interventionist factors (or economic incentives) have a significant impact on the performance of EZs, while the descriptive characteristics (or land use, population, and size) do not have such an impact.

PART TWO

A SINGLE CASE STUDY

CHAPTER VII

EMPLOYMENT IMPACTS ON ZONE RESIDENTS

PORTLAND, OREGON

ZONE RESIDENTS AND PARTICIPATING BUSINESSES

This single case study in Part Two, Chapter VII, takes an important step forward in researching some of the important issues raised in the national study in Part One. The data in Table XIII on page 120 for the North/Northeast (N/NE) Portland Enterprise Zone (EZ) provides information on the kinds and sizes of participating EZ businesses, and on new hires who are zone residents. Most telling about the data is that 67% of all new hires are EZ residents. Nabisco Incorporated is a large-size company with 63% of all new hires who are EZ residents; Blue Bell Potato Chip Company and TYCO Distribution Corporation are medium-size companies with 58% and 89% respectively; and Columbia Aluminum Recycle Company (CARCO) and MARCO Machineworks are small-size companies with 44% and 40% respectively. As you can see, the medium and large-size companies have a great many new hires who are EZ residents. All of the firms are in the industrial sector.

The EZ program has had a positive impact on *vastly expanding* the labor force of these companies. Nabisco is a biscuit bakery plant, which produces cookies and crackers, and has 577 total employees and 168 new hires, with 106 EZ residents who are new hires. Blue Bell is a chips plant, which produces baked and fried snacks, and has 240 total employees and 175 new hires, with 102 EZ residents who are new hires.

TABLE 1

ENTERPRISE ZONE DATA
OF N/NE PORTLAND

Name of Business	First Year	New Hires	EZ Residents	Percent of EZ Residents	Company Employees	Investment in Millions of $	Abatement in Thousands $
Nabisco	1989	168	106	63%	531/46*	59.9	3,520.7
Blue Bell	1990	175	102	58%	240	1.0	70.7
MARCO	1990	5	2	40%	8	.1	8.7
CARCO	1991	25	11	44%	19**	2.7	188.5
TYCO	1992	129	115	89%	130**	10.9	603.8
TOTALS		502	336	67%			

Average wage per new job is $10 hour plus additional benefits (health insurance, sick leave, vacation leave, and retirement).

Average tax abatement total cost per new job created is $5,200. (This does not factor in the benefit of public welfare savings.)

TYCO also has seasonal employees ranging from 0 to 250 in number, which are not apart of the EZ program.

* Full time/part-time.
** Total has been adjusted to account for turnover of full time employees.

Participating EZ Businesses

Nabisco Incorporated is a biscuit bakery plant, which produces cookies and crackers.
Blue Bell Potato Chip Company is a chips plant, which produces baked and fried snacks.
MARCO Machineworks is a small machine shop.
Columbia Aluminum Recycle Company (CARCO) is a recycler of aluminum.
TYCO Distribution Corporation is an international distributor of toys.

MARCO is a small machine shop, and has 8 employees and 5 new hires, with 2 EZ residents who are new hires. CARCO is a recyler of aluminum and has 19 total employees and 25 new hires due to turnover, with 11 EZ residents are new hires. TYCO is an international toys distributor and has 130 full time employees and 129 new hires, with 115 EZ residents who are new hires.

In comparison between companies, the level of investment varies widely. Nabisco has made the largest investment to date, while TYCO has made a medium-to-large investment, with $59.9 million and $10.9 million respectively; and both of these companies have had large growth in their labor forces. On the other hand, Blue Bell has made a small investment of $1.0 million, yet has had a large growth in their labor force; while CARCO has made a higher level investment of $2.7 million, yet has had small growth in their labor force. MARCO has made the smallest investment of $0.1 million and the smallest job growth, since it is a very small company.

Again, these companies have had large expansions in the labor force due to the EZ incentives. Two noteworthy points are (1) that no companies have relocated into the EZ, as most of the participating companies (Nabisco, Blue Bell, MARCO, and CARCO) have *expanded* from within the EZ, while one of the participating companies (TYCO) built a *new* plant, which was an expansion of distribution from its manufacturing plant outside of the zone; and (2) that the type of newly created EZ jobs are primarily blue collar.

The data in this case study on the participating businesses and residents in the Portland EZ takes another step forward in analyzing the impact on employment. The precise number of total new hires versus EZ residents newly hired is very valuable to the field of policy research, and this type of data collection is necessary for a thorough evaluation of any EZ program. Although, some form of data collection is mandated in all 30 of Oregon EZs, N/NE Portland is the only EZ in Oregon that is "mandated by the legislature to collect specific data on EZ residents." More data will be available in the future as the following additional firms have been recently approved as participating businesses: Cintas Corporation, which is an industrial laundry supplier; Oregon Steel Mills, which recycles scrap into steel plate; Romar Transportation Company, which is a transport service of rail and sea containers; and

Silver Eagle Company, which manufactures military trailers and suspension systems. Additionally, Ann Sacks Tile is making future plans on expanding its building and larbor force, and on getting EZ incentives approval.

OREGON LEGISLATION

Three important characteristics of Oregon State EZ legislation are (1) that for Portland, a minimum of 40% of new hires must be EZ residents, although some stipulations on hiring can be waived if a company invests $25 million or more (Also, detailed data collecting and reporting is required and administered through the local EZ manager at the Portland Development Commission); and (2) that there is a first source hiring agreement with a large job referral and training provider (which, for Portland, is the local JOB-NET program with its large training network, including the federal Job Training Partnership Act or JTPA program); and (3) that the legislation provides property tax abatements for construction and renovation.

The Portland mandate on at least 40% of new hires being EZ residents does hinder many service sector businesses from developing, if the companies require highly skilled workers. American Airlines is a firm that chose not to build company offices with 600 employees in the N/NE Portland EZ, due to too many obstacles, including the residential mandate. American Airlines wanted the legislature to grant a waiver to drop the minimum new hire mandate to 30% of EZ residents, so that a large percentage of current employees could be relocated there. This difficult issue along with other serious problems killed the deal. The manufacturing industry with blue collar labor has had a much easier time *meeting* and *exceeding* the new hire mandate of EZ residents, due to the entry level and most common job (blue collar) skills of EZ residents.

The minimum hire mandate in three other urban zones in Oregon is a 50% requirement, but this stipulation includes all of the residents in the metropolitan or regional urban growth boundary. In essence, this mandate is easier to meet. All other zones throughout Oregon, which are chiefly rural, have no residency mandates.

The first source hiring agreement in Portland is a model job referral initiative for EZ programs. JOB-NET has 205 active affiliates, which are widely ranging in organizational mission and scope, from the Oregon State Employment Division and The Urban League of Portland to the Albina Ministerial Alliance and store front churches. Most of the JOB-NET affiliates are *private* organizations. All types of social services are provided in the different affiliates including job contacts, job training, job interviewing skills, and personal grooming as needed. Although, the job referral service may be of greatest value to the EZ residents by securing interviews for all new EZ jobs during the duration of the agreement. However, the zone businesses feel that they incur additional job costs by employing a work force with greater absenteeism and unmotivated employees among the zone residents who are new hires.

Additionally, three metro-area community colleges participate in JOB-NET. The special vocational and technical training program at Portland Community College, the EZ property tax incentive, and especially the State's guarantee of $50 million in speical revenue bonds (financial incentive) were elements in Pacific Air Maintenance Corporation's (PAMCORP's) decision in 1992 to build in Portland. Portland competed with many other western cities for PAMCORP's fleet repair and maintenance of major airlines. Unfortunately, the airline industry as a whole has recently experienced economic hard times, so PAMCORP had to close down operations after a short time and before getting their Portland company fully established.

Another interesting element of this episode is that the Portland International Airport area was also annexed into the EZ, which was a major incentive for PAMCORP. The administrative rules allow for property to be annexed, in proportion to the EZ area (public property and wet land) that is unable to be developed. But residential areas are not allowed to be annexed, so that any business annexation directly benefits EZ residents and the first source hiring provider, creating a win-win situation for the public-private partnership. Also, Oregon Steel Mills has benefitted by this provision.

The property tax incentives are for new construction and renovation, so medium and large-size business with major building, expansion, and renovation projects are the primary beneficiaries. The property tax abatement is for 100% of the assessed value of new construction and renovation for three years.

A qualified firm must increase its employment by 10% in the first year to be eligible for the property tax incentive. If any qualified firm makes a $25 million or more investment and *retains* its existing work force, then the 10% mandate on increasing its work force is waived. Under special circumstances, this last provision on investment can even apply to a firm that has a reduction in the work force.

INCENTIVES PACKAGE AND CROSS-BORDER ACTIVITY

Although the N/NE Portland EZ has been very successful in the hiring of EZ residents per new job created, the author's strong recommendation is that Oregon should amend its current legislation to provide employer income tax incentives to strengthen and broaden the program. The author's national study in Part One shows that both property and income tax incentives when combined for employers have a significant impact on employment, apparently due to the high dollar value contained in these tax incentives. In fact when both property and income tax incentives are combined in a full-scale program, there is an immediate and major impact on employment within a year. Thus, a full-scale EZ program with many incentives, including property and income tax incentives, is best of all and should be adopted by Oregon and all states serious about increasing economic development and employment in poverty areas. This would increase the number of participating businesses, which would increase the hiring of zone residents. This is especially true for small businesses, as more and better economic incentives would increase their productivity, growth, and participation in hiring EZ residents.

In accord with a study on Illinois cited in Part One, Chapter II, greater deregulation is also an important incentive, especially for small business, as shown in the experience of MARCO, which is in the process of backing out of the N/NE Portland EZ program due to the costs of complying with excessive and burdensome administrative rule changes, which occurred after it was approved as a participating business. Thus, the reduction of regulatory procedures and compliance costs would be an important part in any incentives package.

Other incentives in a full-scale package could include personal income tax credits for new hires who are employed through the first source training provider. This would serve as a supplemental incentive to unemployed local residents along with enhancing their job training providers. This would also assist with the personal finances of the unemployed Portland residents in competing for entry level jobs with the commuting Vancouver, Washington residents who would pay Oregon income taxes.

A sales tax incentive in Oregon EZs is unnecessary, since Oregon does not have a sales tax, except on a few items, such as hotel/motel lodging, gasoline, tobacco, and alcohol. Having no sales taxes is already an incentive for retail business in Portland, as consumers from across the river in Washington State commute to make purchases. However, the N/NE Portland EZ boundary does not receive the high retail volume, as do other Portland areas, so retail jobs tend to grow in these other areas. But having no sales taxes is also an incentive for Portland businesses that make large purchases of equipment and supplies for production, and this does include the N/NE Portland EZ.

Actually, a sales tax incentive and EZ program in Vancouver, Washington is greatly needed, as retail business in the downtown area has dwindled over the years, due to the competition from Portland (which has no sales tax) and the attraction of large shopping malls. Retail businesses in downtown Vancouver are finding that paying the sales tax for the customer, which is similar to a reduced sales price, has increased the volume of retailing. In fact, the local newspaper has reported that the Washington State Department of Revenue has estimated that the sales tax could be reduced by about 3% or more (from 7.6% to about 4.6% or so) in Clark County, and still maintain the current level of public revenues, due to the increased retail activity of a lower sales tax by attracting the Vancouver residents who would otherwise shop in Portland. More importantly, legislating (1) employer property tax abatements and (2) employer income (Business and Occupations) tax credits would have a major impact on employment as demonstrated by the author's study. Again, a full-scale incentives package, with property, income, and sales tax incentives among others incentives, would be a redevelopment boom to this urban area.

Oregon EZs should be ready to apply for any available federal incentives, both now and in the future. It may be difficult for an Oregon EZ to receive the income tax incentives available to just nine federally-designated EZs in 1994-95. But the near future promises the creation of federally-sponsored community development banks, which should make available low interest loans to businesses in a great many EZs. Oregon could also move forward with state-sponsored low interest loans to EZ businesses, just as other states have done, to get a head start on combining state and federal financial incentives. Due to the demographics, the N/NE Portland EZ is the most likely in Oregon to compete for and receive this type of federal incentive.

POLICY MANDATES

Two additional and important policy recommendations from this single case study, which should be mandated by federal and state legislatures are: (1) that specific data on all new job hires who are and are not zone residents be derived for all EZ programs; and (2) that a job referral and training network be provided for all EZ programs.

The first recommendation of deriving data on new jobs and zone residents would contribute greatly to program evaluation. Although secondary, demographic information on age, sex, ethnicity, income, education, household dependents, and disability status would increase the knowledge of the impacts on various zone residents. Also, data is needed on EZ business owners, investors, and entrepreneurs in regard to assets (investment capital, earnings, equipment, and facilites), type of industry (manufacturing, distributing, service, and retailing), productivity and the number of employees, and demographics (similar to the data needed on zone residents), which would enhance the knowledge of EZ outcomes. Some of the annual data on business capital investment dollars and the number of new jobs in the state EZs are already derived by HUD.

The second recommendation on providing referral and training networks at the local level would enhance the hiring of zone residents for the newly created jobs. The job referral and training provider networks in Portland and throughout Oregon constitute a model that is largely *privitized* for other states and localities to emulate.

Many businesses throughout the country employ new hires through *informal* employee/personal referrals and social networks, which can obviate the hiring of local residents. Thus, the *formal* referral agreements in Oregon supersede the conventional ways that employers seek out good job applicants. EZ residents in Portland have benefitted greatly by this public-private partnership with a job referral and job training network.

SUMMARY STATEMENT

In conclusion, this single case study is a landmark in beginning research on specific employment outcomes of zone residents. The 67% employment of zone residents for the new jobs is the most significant finding in evaluating the North/Northeast Portland EZ.

APPENDIX A

STATES WITH ENTERPRISE ZONE LEGISLATION*

Alabama (12)
Arizona (11)
Arkansas (458)
California** (34)
Colorado (16)
Connecticut (11)
Delaware (30)
District of Columbia (3)
Florida (30)
Georgia (3)
Hawaii (-)
Illinois (90)
Indiana (15)
Kansas (255)
Kentucky (10)
Louisiana (1,553)
Maine*** (4)
Maryland (17)
Michigan (1)
Minnesota*** (16)

Mississippi*** (25)
Missouri (50)
Nebraska (-)
Nevada (2)
New Jersey (10)
New York (19)
Ohio (227)
Oklahoma (88)
Oregon (30)
Pennsylvania (45)
Rhode Island (5)
South Carolina (3)
Tennessee (2)
Texas (103)
Utah (15)
Vermont (3)
Virginia (18)
West Virginia (-)
Wisconsin (8)

Totals: 38 states and one district with 3,232 zones (zones in parentheses)

Hawaii, Nebraska, and West Virginia are in the process of establishing and designating zones

*   Including Washington, D.C.
**   California has two legislated programs, named after legislators Nolan and Waters
***   Sunset provisions (legislation under review for renewal)

(This data is adapted from the 1992 U.S. Department of Housing and Urban Development summary.)

STATES WITHOUT ENTERPRISE ZONE LEGISLATION

Alaska
Idaho
Iowa
Massachusetts
Montana
New Hampshire
New Mexico
North Carolina
North Dakota
South Dakota
Washington
Wyoming

(12 states)

(This data is adapted from the 1992 U.S. Department of Housing and Urban Development summary.)

APPENDIX B

KEY QUESTIONS ON SURVEY

PART 1. LOCAL ZONE CHARACTERISTICS AND PERFORMANCE

Questions:

1. *What is the name of the State-designated Enterprise Zone?*
2. *What is the name of the community in which the Zone is located?*
3. *When was the area designated as a State Enterprise Zone? (month/day/year)*

Socio-Demographic Data on Community and Zone:

	At Designation		Current	
	Zone	*Community*	*Zone*	*Community*

5. *Population*
6. *% Unemployment*

Land Use:
10. *How many square miles in the designated Zone?*
11. *How is land used in the Zone?*
    Percent of Land in Zone
    a. *Residential*
    b. *Commercial*
    c. *Industrial*
    d. *Open Space*
    e. *Other*

(This appendix is adapted from Part 1, Page 3, of the survey instrument used by the U.S. Department of Housing and Urban Development. Please note that some of the questions have been skipped in the adaptation, due to irrelevancy or incompletion in the data base.)

REFERENCES

American Legislative Exchange Council (1993). "Voting With Their Feet II: The Economic Consequences of Cross-Border Activity in the Southeastern U.S.." *The State Factor.* Tax and Fiscal Policy Task Force. August 1993.

Armey, Dick (1992). "Small Business and the Recession." *The Wall Street Journal.* November 6, 1992. Page A14. (This article by Congressman Armey summarizes a study for the Joint Economic Committee of the U.S. Congress.)

Bates, Timothy (1993). *Banking on Black Enterprise: The Potential of Emerging Firms for Revitalizing Urban Economies.* Published by the Joint Center for Political and Economic Studies, Washington, D.C.. Distributed by University Press of America, Lanham, Maryland.

Benson, Bruce L. (1986). "Do Taxes Matter? The Impact of State and Local Taxes on Economic Development." *Economic Development Commentary* (Winter 1986). Vol. 10, No. 4, pp. 4-7.

Brintall, Michael and Green, Roy E. (1988). "Comparing State Enterprise Zone Programs: Variations in Structure and Coverage." *Economic Development Quarterly.* Vol. 2; pp. 58-68.

_____ (1991). "Framework for a Comparative Analysis of State-Administered Enterprise Zone Programs." *Enterprise Zones: New Directions in Economic Development.* Ed. Roy E. Green. Newbury Park, CA: Sage Publications; Ch. 5, pp. 75-88.

Brookes, Warren T. (1982). *The Economy in Mind.* New York, N.Y.: Universe Books. (This work was sponsored by the Manhattan Institute for Policy Research.)

Business Facilities (1985-92). Feature: Enterprise Zones. Each May issue. (These annual articles feature net jobs and investments in all Enterprise Zones.)

Butler, John Shipley (1991). *Entrepreneurship and Self-Help Among Black Americans: A Reconsideration of Race and Economics.* Albany, New York: State University of New York Press.

Butler, Stuart M. (1980). "Enterprise Zones: Pioneering in the Inner City." In *Critical Issues*, Washington, D.C.: The Heritage Foundation.

_____ (1981). *Enterprise Zones: Greenlining the Inner Cities.* New York, N.Y.: Universe Books. (Dr. Butler's seminal work also refers to the research of David Birch of the Massachusetts Institute of Technology where businesses and jobs are lost at the same rate in all cities throughout the nation, but that businesses and jobs are created, replaced, and expanded at a greater rate than their losses in the communities with dynamic, small business development.)

_____ (1982a). "Enterprise Zone Update." In *Issue Bulletin* (November 29, 1982). Washington, D.C.: The Heritage Foundation.

_____ (1982b). "The Enterprise Zone Tax Act of 1982: The Administration Plan." In *Issue Bulletin* (March 29, 1982). Washington, D.C.: The Heritage Foundation.

_____ (1983). "Enterprise Zones: Time to Act." In *Issue Bulletin* (November 17, 1983). Washington, D.C. The Heritage Foundation.

_____ (1989). "How to Design Effective Enterprise Zone Legislation." In *The Heritage Lectures* (No. 215). Washington, D.C.: The Heritage Foundation.

_____ (1991). "The Conceptual Evolution of Enterprise Zones. " *Enterprise Zones: New Directions in Economic Development.* Ed. Roy E. Green. Newbury Park, CA: Sage Publications, Ch. 2, pp. 27-40.

Colson, Chuck and Eckerd, Jack (1991). *Why America Doesn't Work.* Dallas, Texas: Word Publishing.

Dabney, Dan Y. (1991). "Do Enterprise Zone Incentives Affect Business Location Decisions?" *Economic Development Quarterly.* November 1991. Vol. 5, No. 4: pp. 325-334.

Daubon, Ramon E. and Villamil (1991). "Puerto Rico as an Enterprise Zone." *Enterprise Zones: New Directions in Economic Development.* Ed. Roy E. Green. Newbury Park, CA: Sage Publications; Ch. 13, pp. 207-222.

Davidson, James Dale and Rees-Mogg, Lord William (1991). *The Great Reckoning: How the World will Change in the Depression of the 1990s.* New York, N.Y.: Summit Books.

Davies, Christie (1992). "Moralization and Demoralization: A Moral Explanation for Changes in Crime, Disorder and Social Problems." *The Loss of Virtue: Moral Confusion and Social Disorder in Britain and America.* Edited by Digby Anderson. United States of America: The Social Affairs Unit, A National Review Book; Chapter 1, pp.1-13.

Elling, Richard C. and Sheldon Ann Workman (1991). "Determinants of Enterprise Zone Success: A Four State Perspective. *Enterprise Zones: New Directions in Economic Development.* Ed. Roy E. Green. Newbury Park, CA: Sage Publications; Ch. 9, pp. 136-154.

Enterprise Zones: New Directions in Economic Development (1991). Ed. Roy E. Green. Newbury Park, CA: Sage Publications

Erickson, Rodney A., and Friedman, Susan W. (1991). "Comparative Dimensions of State Enterprise Zone Policies." *Enterprise Zones: New Directions in Economic Development.* Ed. Roy E. Green. Newbury Park, CA: Sage Publications; Ch. 10, pp. 155-176.

Erickson, Rodney A., and Friedman, Susan W., McCluskey, Richard E. (1989). *Enterprise Zones: An Evaluation of State Government Policies.* (Final Report to the U.S. Department of Commerce, Economic Development Administration, Technical Assistance and Research Division.)

Esparza, Adrian and Williams, Martin (1990). "Regional Job Creation Policies: The Empirical Evidence for Illinois Enterprise Zones." *Review of Urban and Regional Development Studies* (July 1990). Vol. 2, No. 2, pp. 163-173.

Freeman, Richard B. (1986). "The Relationship of Churchgoing and Other Background Factors to the Socio-economic Performance of Black Male Youths from Inner City Tracts." *The Black Youth Employment Crisis.* Eds. Richard B. Freeman and Harry J. Holzer. Chicago: University of Chicago Press.

Frey, James H. (1983). *Survey Research by Telephone.* Beverly Hills, CA: Sage Publications.

Friedman, Milton and Rose (1979). *Free to Choose.* New York, N.Y.: Avon Publications, a division of The Hearst Corporation. Pages 102-103.

Grasso, Patrick G. and Crosse, Scott B. (1991). "Enterprise Zones: Maryland Case Study." *Enterprise Zones: New Directions in Economic Development.* Ed. Roy E. Green. Newbury Park, CA: Sage Publications; Ch. 8, pp. 122-135.

Green, Roy E. (1990). "Is There a Place in the 1990s for Federally Designated Enterprise Zones within the Context of State-administered Enterprise Zone Program Experience?" *Journal of Planning Literature.* Vol. 5, pp. 38-45.

Green, Shelley and Pryde, Jr., Paul (1989). *Black Entrepreneurship in America.* New Brunswick, New Jersey: Transactions Publishers, Rutgers University.

Grunwald, Joseph (1991). "Assembly Industries, Technology Transfer, and Enterprise Zones." *Enterprise Zones: New Directions in Economic Development.* Ed. Roy E. Green. Newbury Park, CA: Sage Publications; Ch. 12. pp. 192-206.

Gusskind, Robert (1990). "Enterprise Zones: Do They Work?" *Journal of Housing.* January/February 1990. Vol. 47, No. 1: pp. 47-54.

Hall, Peter (1991). "British Enterprise Zones." *Enterprise Zones: New Directions in Economic Development.* Ed. Roy E. Green. Newbury Park, CA: Sage Publications; Ch. 11, pp. 179-191.

Hansen, Susan B. (1991). "Comparing Enterprise Zones to Other Economic Development Techniques." *Enterprise Zones: New Directions in Economic Development.* Ed. Roy. E. Green. Newbury Park, CA.: Sage Publications, Ch. 1, pp. 7-26.

Hertel, Bradley R. and Hughes, Michael (1987). "Religious Affiliation, Attendance, and Support for 'Pro-Family' Issues in the United States." *Social Forces.* Vol. 65, No. 3. pp. 858-882.

Hirsch, Werner Z. (1984). *Urban Economics.* New York, N.Y.: Macmillan Publishing Company.

Jacobs, Jane (1961). *The Death and Life of Great American Cities.* New York, N.Y.: Vintage Books.

Kemp, Jack (1984). *The American Idea: Ending Limits to Growth.* Washington, D.C.: The American Studies Center.

Klemens, Michael D. (1991). "Enterprise Zones: Do They Work as Economic Development Tools?" *Illinois Issues.* August/September 1991. Vol. 17, Nos. 8/9: pp. 26-27.

Limbaugh, Rush (1992). *The Way Things Ought To Be.* New York, N.Y.: Pocket Books, a division of Simon and Schuster, Inc..

Logan, Jr., Willie and Barron, Lee Ann (1991). "Florida's Enterprise Zone Program: The Program after Sunset." *Enterprise Zones: New Directions in Economic Development.* Ed. Roy. E. Green. Newbury Park, CA.: Sage Publications, Ch. 6, pp. 91-104.

Lowry, Glenn C. (1993). "God and the Ghetto." *The Wall Street Journal.* February 26, 1993. Page A14. (This article by Economics Professor Lowry at Boston University reviews academic research on the issue of moral values versus economic and public policy factors in regard to family and community life in black ghettos.)

Mansfield, Edwin (1990). *Managerial Economics: Theory, Applications, and Cases.* New York, N.Y.: W. W. Norton & Company.

Mellor, Herman A. (1987). "Conservative Policy and the Poor: Enterprise Zones." *Steering the Elephant: How Washington Works.* Eds. Robert Rector and Michael Sanera. New York, N.Y.: Universe Books, Ch. 19, pp. 198-215.

Mills, Edwin S. (1987). "The Determinants of Small Area Growth." *Lectures in Economics.* University Graduate Faculty of Economics. Lecture Series #1. October 1987. Oregon State University.

Moore, Stephen and Stansel, Dean (1993). "The Myth of America's Underfunded Cities." *Policy Analysis.* No. 188; February 22, 1993. Washington, D.C.: The Cato Institute.

Murphy, Cait (1986). "Around the States: EZ Does It." *Policy Review* (Spring 1986). No. 36. Washington, D.C.: The Heritage Foundation.

Murray, Charles A. (1984). *Losing Ground: American Social Policy 1950-80.* New York, N.Y.: Basic Books Inc..

Murray, Charles A. (1993). "The Coming White Underclass." _The Wall Street Journal._ October 29, 1993, Page A12.

National Association of State Development Agencies. _NASDA Letter, The._ Special Issue (November 4, 1985). Washington, D.C..

Nicholson, Walter (1992). _Microeconomic Theory: Basic Principles and Extensions._ Fifth Edition. Fort Worth, Tx.: The Dryden Press, a division of Harcourt Brace Jovanovich College Publishers.

Pierce, Samuel R., Jr. (1986). "Enterprise Zones Three Years Later." _Economic Development Commentary_ (Winter 1986). Vol. 10, No. 4, pp. 4-7.

Price-Waterhouse (1992). "Voting with Their Feet: A Study of Tax Incentives and Economic Consequences of Cross-Border Activity in New England." _The State Factor._ American Legislative Exchange Council. August 1992. (This is the first part of a two-part series.)

Pryde, Jr., Paul (1987). "Investing in People: A New Approach to Job Creation." _On the Road to Economic Freedom._ Ed. Robert. L Woodson. Washington, D.C.: Regnery Gateway. (Mr. Pryde has also authored a three-volume monograph on the federal role in economic development, entitled, _Development Finance: A Primer for Policy Makers_, plus numerous publications on business and community development finance.)

Redfield, Kent D. and McDonald, John F. (1991). _Enterprise Zones in Illinois._ Illinois Tax Foundation. August 1991. (This was a study conducted for the Illinois Tax Foundation by the Institute for Public Affairs, Sangamon State University, Springfield, Illinois.)

Reichley, A. James (1985). _Religion in American Public Life._ Washington, D.C.: Brookings Institute.

Rothenberg, Jerome (1967). _Economic Evaluation of Urban Renewal._ Washington, D.C.: The Brookings Institute.

Roberts, Paul Craig (1983). _The Supply-side Revolution._ Cambridge, Massachusetts: Harvard University Press.

Rubenstein, David (1992). "Don't Blame Crime on Joblessness." *The Wall Street Journal.* November 9, 1992. Page A14. (This article by Professor Rubenstein of the University of Illinois at Chicago summarizes scholarly research on the anomalies of poverty causing crime.)

Rubin, B.M. and M.G. Wilder (1989). "Urban Enterprise Zones: Employment Impacts and Fiscal Incentives." *Journal of the American Planning Association.* Fall 1989. Vol. 55, No. 4: pp. 418-431.

Rubin, Marilyn Marks (1990). "Urban Enterprise Zones, Do They Work? Evidence from New Jersey." *Public Budgeting and Finance.* Winter 1990. Vol. 10, No. 4: pp. 3-17.

_____(1991). "Urban Enterprise Zones in New Jersey: Have They Made a Difference?" *Enterprise Zones: New Directions in Economic Development.* Ed. Roy E. Green. Newbury Park, CA: Sage Publications; Ch. 7, pp. 105-121.

Rubin, Marilyn Marks and Trawinski, Edward J. (1991). "New Jersey's Urban Enterprise Zones: A Program that Works." *The Urban Lawyer.* Vol. 23, No. 3: pp. 461-471.

Schmidt Ronald H. (1993). "Regional Comparative Advantage." *FRBSF Weekly Letter.* Research Department. Federal Reserve Bank of San Francisco. Number 93-37. October 29, 1993.

Sennholz, Hans F. (1987). *The Politics of Unemployment.* Spring Mills, PA: Libertarian Press, Inc.

Stack Steven (1983). "The Effect of the Decline of Institutionalized Religion on Suicide, 1954-78." *Journal for the Scientific Study of Religion.* Vol. 22; pp. 239-252.

Sullivan, Arthur M. (1990). *Urban Economics.* Boston, Massachusetts: Richard D. Irwin, Inc..

Tucker, Jeffrey A. (1991). "EZ Living: Enterprise Zones and the Welfare State." *Chronicles.* June 1991, pp. 46-49.

U.S. Congress (1992). Joint Economic Committee. *Derailing the Small Business Job Express*. Report prepared for Representative Richard Armey (R-TX), Ranking Republican. November 7, 1992. (This study was authored by Lowell Gallaway of Ohio University and Gary Anderson of California State University, Northridge.)

U.S. Department of Housing and Urban Development (1986). *State-Designated Enterprise Zones: Ten Case Studies*. Office of Program Analysis and Evaluation. Washington, D.C.: U.S. Government Printing Office.

_____ (1988). *Fact Sheet*. Washington, D.C..

_____ (1992). *State Enterprise Zone Update: Summaries of the State Enterprise Programs*. Office of Community Planning and Development. Washington, D.C.: U.S. Government Printing Office. (At present, HUD has not issued a 1993 summary update.)

U.S. General Accounting Office, Program Evaluation and Methodology Division (1988). *Lessons from the Maryland Experience*. Washington, D.C.: U.S. Government Printing Office.

U.S. Library of Congress (1992a). Congressional Research Service. *Enterprise Zones: The Design of Tax Incentives*. Report No. 92-476, by Jane G. Gravelle. Washington D.C., June 3, 1992.

_____ (1992b). Congressional Research Service. *Enterprise Zones: A Comparison of House, Senate, and Administration Bills in the 102nd Congress*. Report No. 92-654 E, by J. F. Hornbeck. Washington, D.C., August 13, 1992.

Vedder, Richard K. (1993). "The Economic Impact of an Oregon Sales Tax." *Fiscal Insight #7*. Cascade Policy Institute. October 1993.

Vedder, Richard and Gallaway, Lowell (1992). "Why Johnny Can't Work: The Causes of Unemployment." *Policy Review*. No. 62. Fall 1992, pp. 24-30.

_____ (1993). *Out of Work: Unemployment and Government in Twentieth Century America*. New York, N.Y.: Holmes and Meier, Publishers. (This study was authored for the Independent Institute in Oakland, California.)

Verstanding, Lee L. (1985). "Enterprise Zones Revisited: The Entrepreneurial Spirit." In *Legislative Policy*. Washington, D.C.: U.S. Department of Housing and Urban Development.

Wall Street Journal, The (1993). "Black Entrepreneurship." The Wall Street Journal Reports. Friday, February 19, 1993. (This supplemental section includes information on both capital formation and Enterprise Zones.)

Waltzman, Rick (1992). *The Wall Street Journal*. Politics and Policy, page A16 (September 1, 1992). (This article outlined recent federal EZ proposals by both houses of congress and the executive branch.)

Wanniski, Jude (1989). *The Way the World Works*. Morristown, New Jersey: Polyconomics, Inc..

Watson, Donald S. (1991). *Price Theory and Its Uses*. Fifth Edition. Lanham, Maryland: University Press of America.

Wilson, William Julius (1987). *The Truly Disadvantaged: The Inner City, the Underclass, and Public Policy*. Chicago, Illinois: University of Chicago Press.

Wolf, Michael Allan (1989a). "An 'Essay in Re-Plan': American Enterprise Zones in Practice." *The Urban Lawyer: The National Quarterly in Local Government Law (Winter 1989)*. Vol. 21, No. 1. American Bar Association.

_____ (1989b) "Setting the EZ Record Straight: What Can We Learn from the States." In *Tax Notes* (March 27, 1989), pp. 1657-1660.

_____ (1990) "Enterprise Zones: A Decade of Diversity." Commentary. *Economic Development Quarterly*. February 1990. Vol. 4, No. 1, pp. 3-14.

_____ (1991). "Enterprise Zones through the Legal Looking-Glass." *Enterprise Zones: New Directions in Economic Development*. Ed. Roy E. Green. Newbury Park, CA: Sage Publications; Ch. 4, pp. 58-74.

Woodson, Robert L. (1987). *On the Road to Economic Freedom: An Agenda for Black Progress*. Ed. Robert L. Woodson. Washington, D.C.: Regnery Gateway. (Mr. Woodson is the Founder and President of the National Center for Neighborhood Enterprise.)

Zinsmeister, Karl (1992).   "The Murphy Brown Question: Do Children Need
    Fathers?"   *Crisis*.   October 1992, pp. 21-24.   (This article was originally a
    testimony given before the National Commission on America's Urban
    Families.   Mr. Zinsmeister is an adjunct scholar at the American Enterprise
    Institute.)

INDEX

(geographical, legal, organizational and person index)

ABOUT THE AUTHOR

Terry Wm. Van Allen, Ph.D., is the Director of Research Initiatives at the University of Houston--Clear Lake. Previously, Dr. Van Allen was the Training Director of Public Administration and Policy, and Academic Administrator/Grants Officer of the University Affiliated Program at The Oregon Health Sciences University where he conducted the research for this two-part book. Dr. Van Allen earned his doctorate in Public Administration and Policy at the School of Urban and Public Affairs, Portland State University. He has also taught at Pacific University, Principia College, and Lee College.

Dr. Van Allen was a Salvatori Fellow for "Leadership in Excellence in Higher Education" at The Heritage Foundation, Washington, D.C., a public policy think tank. He has also received the IDEAS Award from the U.S. Department of Housing and Urban Development, Portland, Oregon.